e-Learning in FE

Other Titles in the Essential FE Toolkit Series

Books for Lecturers

Teaching the FE Curriculum – Mark Weyers

e-Learning in FE – John Whalley, Theresa Welch and Lee Williamson

FE Lecturer's Survival Guide – Angela Steward

FE Lecturer's Guide to Diversity and Inclusion – Anne-Marie Wright, Sue Colquhoun, Sina Abdi-Jama, Jane Speare and Tracey Partridge.

How to Manage Stress in FE – Elizabeth Hartney

Guide to Teaching 14–19 – James Ogunleye

Ultimate FE Lecturer's Handbook – Ros Clow and Trevor Dawn

A to Z of Teaching in FE – Angela Steward

Getting the Buggers Motivated in FE – Sue Wallace

Books for Managers

Everything you Need to Know About FE Policy – Yvonne Hillier

Middle Management in FE – Ann Briggs

Managing Higher Education in Colleges – Gareth Parry, Anne Thompson and Penny Blackie

Survival Guide for College Managers and Leaders – David Collins

Guide to Leadership and Governance in FE – Adrian Perry

Guide to Financial Management in FE – Julian Gravatt

Guide to Race Equality in FE – Beulah Ainley

Ultimate FE Leadership and Management Handbook – Jill Jameson and Ian McNay

A to Z for Every Manager in FE – Susan Wallace and Jonathan Gravells

Guide to VET – Christopher Winch and Terry Hyland

e-Learning in FE

John Whalley, Theresa Welch
and Lee John Williamson

continuum

Continuum International Publishing Group

The Tower Building   80 Maiden Lane, Suite 704
11 York Road   New York
SE1 7NX   NY 10038

www.continuumbooks.com

British Library Cataloguing-in-Publication Data
A catalogue record for this book is available from the British Library.

ISBN: 0–8264–8862–5 (paperback)

Library of Congress Cataloging-in-Publication Data
A catalog record for this book is available from the Library of Congress.

Typeset by YHT Ltd
Printed and bound in Great Britain by, Ashford Colour Press Ltd, Gosport, Hampshire.

Contents

Series foreword

THE ESSENTIAL FE TOOLKIT SERIES

Jill Jameson
Series Editor

In the autumn of 1974, a young woman newly arrived from Africa landed in Devon to embark on a new life in England. Having travelled half way round the world, she still longed for sunny Zimbabwe. Not sure what career to follow, she took a part-time job teaching EFL to Finnish students. Having enjoyed this, she studied thereafter for a PGCE at the University of Nottingham in Ted Wragg's Education Department. After teaching in secondary schools, she returned to university in Cambridge, and, after graduating, took a job in ILEA in 1984 in adult education. She loved it: there was something about adult education that woke her up, made her feel fully alive, newly aware of all the lifelong learning journeys being followed by so many students and staff around her. The adult community centre she worked in was a joyful place for diverse multi-ethnic communities. Everyone was cared for, including 90-year-olds in wheelchairs, toddlers in the crèche, ESOL refugees, city accountants in business suits and university level graphic design students. In her eyes, the centre was an educational ideal, a remarkable place in which, gradually, everyone was helped to learn to be who they wanted to be. This was the Chequer Centre, Finsbury, EC1, the 'red house', as her daughter saw it, toddling in from the crèche. And so began the story of a long interest in further education that was to last for many years . . . why, if they did such good work for so many, were FE centres so under-funded and unrecognized, so under-appreciated?

It is with delight that, 32 years after the above story began, I write the Foreword to *The Essential FE Toolkit*, Continuum's new series of 24 books on further education (FE) for teachers and college leaders. The idea behind the *Toolkit* is to provide a comprehensive guide to FE in a series of compact, readable books. The suite of 24 individual books are gathered together to provide the practitioner with an overall FE toolkit in specialist, fact-filled volumes designed to be easily accessible, written by experts with significant knowledge and experience in their individual fields. All of the authors have in-depth understanding of further education. But 'Why is further education important? Why does it merit a whole series to be written about it?' you may ask.

At the Association of Colleges Annual Conference in 2005, in a humorous speech to college principals, John Brennan said that, whereas in 1995 further education was a 'political backwater', by 2005 it had become 'mainstream'. John recalled that since 1995 there had been '36 separate Government or Government-sponsored reports or white papers specifically devoted to the post-16 sector'. In our recent regional research report (2006) for the Learning and Skills Development Agency, my co-author Yvonne Hillier and I noted that it was no longer 'raining policy' in FE, as we had described earlier (Jameson and Hillier, 2003): there is now a torrent of new initiatives. We thought in 2003 that an umbrella would suffice to protect you. We'd now recommend buying a boat to navigate these choppy waters, as it looks as if John Brennan's 'mainstream' FE, combined with a tidal wave of government policies will soon lead to a flood of new interest in the sector, rather than end anytime soon.

There are good reasons for all this government attention on further education. In 2004/2005, student numbers in LSC-funded further education increased to 4.2m, total college income was around £6.1 billion, and the average college had an annual turnover of £15m. Further education has rapidly increased in national significance regarding the need for ever greater achievements in UK education and skills training for millions of learners, providing qualifications and workforce training to feed a UK national economy hungrily in competition with other OECD nations. The 120 recommendations of the Foster Review (2005) therefore in the main encourage colleges to focus their work on vocational skills, social inclusion and achieving academic progress. This series is here to consider all three of these areas and more.

The series is written for teaching practitioners, leaders and managers in the 572 FE/LSC-funded institutions in the UK, including FE colleges, adult education and sixth form institutions, prison education departments, training and workforce development units, local education authorities and community agencies. The series is also written for PGCE/Cert Ed/City & Guilds Initial and continuing professional development (CPD) teacher trainees in universities in the UK, USA, Canada, Australia, New Zealand and beyond. It will also be of interest to staff in the 600 Jobcentre Plus providers in the UK and to many private training organisations. All may find this series of use and interest in learning about FE educational practice in the 24 different areas of these specialist books from experts in the field.

Our use of this somewhat fuzzy term 'practitioners' includes staff in the FE/LSC-funded sector who engage in professional practice in governance, leadership, management, teaching, training, financial and administration services, student support services, ICT and MIS technical support, librarianship, learning resources, marketing, research and development, nursery and crèche services, community and business support, transport and estates management. It is also intended to include staff in a host of other FE services including work-related training, catering, outreach and specialist health, diagnostic additional learning support, pastoral and religious support for students. Updating staff in professional practice is critically important at a time of such continuing radical policy-driven change, and we are pleased to contribute to this nationally and internationally.

We are also privileged to have an exceptional range of authors writing for the series. Many of our series authors are renowned for their work in further education, having worked in the sector for thirty years or more. Some have received OBE or CBE honours, professorships, fellowships and awards for contributions they have made to further education. All have demonstrated a commitment to FE that makes their books come alive with a kind of wise guidance for the reader. Sometimes this is tinged with world-weariness, sometimes with sympathy, humour or excitement. Sometimes the books are just plain clever or a fascinating read, to guide practitioners of the future who will read these works. Together, the books make up a considerable portfolio of assets for you to take with you through your journeys in further education. We hope the experience of reading the books will be interesting, instructive and pleasurable and that experience gained from them will last, renewed, for many seasons.

It has been wonderful to work with all of the authors and with Continuum's UK Education Publisher, Alexandra Webster, on this series. The exhilarating opportunity of developing such a comprehensive toolkit of books probably comes once in a lifetime, if at all. I am privileged to have had this rare opportunity, and I thank the publishers, authors and other contributors to the series for making these books come to life with their fantastic contributions to FE.

Dr Jill Jameson
Series Editor
March, 2006

Series introduction

e-Learning in FE: John Whalley, Theresa Welch and Lee John Williamson

Are you wondering how to achieve excellent integration of ICT into your lessons? Are you worried about using e-learning techniques? Are you a bit unsure if you are stretching your FE students enough in lessons?

This essential new guide to e-learning in further education provides an excellent overview of practical ways of including ICT in FE, outlining a wide range of useful techniques, tips, tools and strategies for using e-learning in the FE classroom. In 2005, with the help of BECTA (the British Educational Communications and Technology Agency), Continuum asked expert e-learning guides John Whalley, Theresa Welch and Lee John Williamson and to put together this fascinating practical handbook for teachers. *e-Learning in FE* will enable you to extend opportunities for excellent teaching and learning in your classroom in a range of useful ways, without harming your pocket or making you panic. e-learning techniques are carefully explained in a useful, humorous, comprehensive step-by-step process which talks us through the achievement of successful ICT integration in the classroom.

John, Lee and Theresa begin this useful guide by saying by analysing 'the trouble with FE' in terms of the pressures and bureaucratic challenges facing staff and the difficulties of embracing demands like the constant pressure to include ICT in teaching and learning. However, the authors encourage us to recognize that we need to accept life is changing. Computers are ubiquitous; e-learning is now a necessity, not a luxury, for the FE classroom. FE lecturers now *must* come to terms with the use of e-learning, whether they like it or not.

Given this necessity, the authors aim to help us enjoy and be inspired by e-learning. They provide fascinating practical examples and tips that FE lecturers will find invaluable, exploding a range of myths to encourage confidence in using ICT. The authors provide us with a 'jargon busting' glossary to the wide array of acronyms in e-learning, explaining how, from everyday programs such as Word, Excel and Powerpoint, you can create fascinating resource materials, including drop boxes, quizzes, automatic marking with feedback and using sound and images.

Looking 'inside the digital classroom', John, Theresa and Lee guide us through an overview of the range of activities under the umbrella of e-learning, including 'the e-Teacher's palette', the use of the internet for facts and figures, learning packs, smartboards, digital cameras, mobile phone learning resources and a survival toolkit of learning resources for FE. They introduce us to a range of national and regional organisations supporting the use of e-learning in FE, including BECTA, FERL, JISC, the National Learning Network and TechDis.

The authors guide us through the use of free educational resource materials and shared learning repositories. They also give an overview of Education and Disability Legislation relating to e-learning and advise on the importance of catering for students with disabilities and different learning styles. Pointing to 'what's on the horizon', John, Theresa and Lee show us the way to take advantage of the numerous opportunities available to FE lecturers in e-learning for the future, providing an extensive range of links and further information. This brilliant guide will tell you everything you need to know about *e-Learning in FE* and will also help you to apply it in practice in your own classroom! I highly recommend it to you.

Dr Jill Jameson
Director of Research
School of Education and Training
University of Greenwich
j.jameson@gre.ac.uk

Introduction

This book takes a look at e-learning within Post-16 education in the United Kingdom from a largely practical perspective. It does not aim to be a fully comprehensive guide to all aspects of e-learning, but instead tries to take a practical look at e-learning as it can be used by most teachers and trainers within the sector. It does not try to be a technical manual on all the various manifestations of e-learning since, as will be seen, e-learning can mean many things to many people. What it does try to do is to supply the basics of what most lecturers and trainers could use within their subject areas to get them started with integrating e-learning into their own subject deliveries. Very little technical knowledge is assumed, as one of our aims is to show how e-learning can be used by everyone in the sector and not just the techno-whizzes!

E-learning is a much-quoted phrase in Post-16 education and one which, unfortunately, seems to be regarded by some institutions as having either been embedded or as something that they can now move on from. In a way, it seems strange to refer to 'e-learning' as a discrete entity. In the dim and distant days when I first began lecturing (and believe me, it was a long time ago!), we used to use a machine for copying handouts that consisted of a special sheet of paper that was wrapped around a metal drum. It was then hand-rolled to produce (often smudged) copies for handing out to students. This was called a banda machine and at one time it must have been the cutting-edge of technology. However, I never heard any of my colleagues coming into the staff room and proclaiming 'I'm just off to do some "banda-learning" with my students today'. It would have sounded ridiculous! So why do we readily talk about e-learning as if it is some special beast that we keep trapped in our computers to bring out to perform in front of our students?

E-learning is often seen to be an addition to standard teaching, as many staff tend to think that an in-depth knowledge of programs and computer hardware is required. However, once you start looking at e-learning as an integrated part of your teaching toolkit instead of an add-on, it is quite surprising how far you can go with just a few simple techniques. This book will show you the simple tools and techniques that can send you off down the e-learning route and, hopefully, you will want to find out more. Time is a commodity which is in short supply in Post-16 education and we hope that this book will help you to add interactivity, differentiation and interest to your work in quick and easy ways.

One major aspect we shall be looking at is how you can get a lot out of the applications that you already know about and how the new tools that are becoming increasingly available to us can be used. The Web itself can be a major source of help and materials – provided you know where to look – and we aim to point you in the right direction so that you can quickly benefit from the excellent websites and online resources that are available to teachers and trainers.

Such is the speed of development that between our writing the book and your reading it, there will have been further additions, enhancements and some brand new materials. It may even be that 'the latest thing' has become 'old hat'. Some changes are much slower, however, and this has to do with implementing and following through strategic objectives. After a Virtual Learning Environment (VLE) is introduced into an institution, for example, it can take years to become embedded, particularly when staff development and training has to be squeezed in and around the daily organizational activity, such as teaching. So we shall also be considering these broader strategic issues against the cultural backdrop of Post-16 education.

Our ultimate aim is to bring you to a point where you stop thinking of e-learning as a separate item, where it is as much a part of your everyday delivery as using a whiteboard or overhead projector is at present. If we can start to remove the 'e' from e-learning, then ultimately we will be heading down the right track to enable our students to learn more effectively.

Explanation of key terms used in the book

Below is a list of the main acronyms and abbreviations used throughout the text. We hope it will be an easy reference point so that your reading of the text is not interrupted too much by wondering 'What on earth does that mean?'

3G	Third Generation Technology
ACL	Adult and Community Learning
ALEs	Augmented Learning Environments – an extended VLE
ALT	Association of Learning Technology
Athens	An access management system to Web-based services
BECTA	British Educational Communications and Technology Agency
Blog	Web Log – website for posting messages with the newest at the top, focusing on specific topics
BTEC	Business and Technology Education Council
CAD	Computer-aided Design
CD-RW	Re-writable Compact Disk
CHEST	Combined Higher Education Software Team – supplies IT-related software, data, information and training materials to educational institutions
COSHH	Control of Substances Hazardous to Health
DDA	*Disability Discrimination Act 1995*
DfES	Department for Education and Skills
EEBO	Early English Books Online
e-learning	Learning that is delivered using Information Technology
ESOL	English for Speakers of Other Languages
FE	Further Education
Ferl	Further Education Resources for Learning – a web-based information service for the post-compulsory education sector on the use of ICT and e-learning
FOSS	Free and Open Source Software
GIS	Geographic Information Systems – a smart mapping tool

GPS	Global Positioning System
HE	Higher Education
HTML	Hypertext Markup Language – the language behind Web pages
ICT	Information and Communication(s) Technology – using technology to process and manage information
ILP	Individual Learning Plan
ILT	Information and Learning Technologies – using information technology within education
Intranet	Internal Net – network that is private to a specific organization
iPod	A brand of portable media player
IT	Information Technology
JANET	Joint Academic NETwork
JISC	Joint Information Systems Committee – provides strategic guidance, advice and opportunities in using ICT
KSR	Key Skills Registration
LCD	Liquid Crystal Display
LEA	Local Education Authority
LED	Light Emitting Diode
LSN	Learning and Skills Network
MINTEL	Market research organization
MIS	Management Information Systems – usually used in FE to refer to electronic administration systems and network management
m-learning	Mobile-learning – delivery of learning by means of mobile devices such as PDAs
MLE	Managed Learning Environment – information systems and processes of a college, including its VLE integrated into one system
MMS	Multimedia Messaging Service – mobile phone service used to transmit multimedia content such as video clips
NIACE	National Institute of Adult Continuing Education
NLN	National Learning Network – a national partnership programme designed to increase the uptake of information and learning technology across FE
OHP	Overhead Projector
OSS Watch	Open Source Software Watch
PC	Personal Computer
PDA	Personal Digital Assistant – a hand-held computer used for transmitting
PDF	Portable Document Format – Adobe Acrobat file type

RDN	Resource Discovery Network
RSC	Regional Support Centres of the JISC
SD card	Secure Digital card – a data storage card
SENDA	*Special Educational Needs and Disabilities Act 2001*
SMS	Short Message Service – used on mobile phones; 'texting'
Tablet PC	A portable, slate-shaped computer that allows users to enter information via a stylus
TASI	Technical Advisory Service for Images
TechDis	Advisory service on accessability and inclusion for disabled students and staff in HE and FE
TFT	Thin Film Transistor
UKERNA	United Kingdom Education and Research Networking Association
UKOLN	UK Office for Library Networking
USB	Universal Serial Bus – a way of plugging things into your computer
VLE	Virtual Learning Environment – software which allows teachers and trainers to manage students on a network or over the Web
VTS	Virtual Training Suite
WiFi	Wireless Fidelity – used to connect portable devices to each other and to the Internet
Wiki	An interactive website that anyone can add, edit or remove items from without having to register, useful for collaborative learning.

1 Winning the argument

If you have attended any kind of e-learning seminar or conference recently then you will have heard this one. It's been doing the rounds for a while but is worth repeating:

> Did you hear the one about the train driver, the surgeon and the teacher?
>
> They were all working happily in Victorian England when suddenly they get sucked into a vortex and land in the year 2006. When they turn up for work the next day, they are shocked.
>
> The train driver cannot drive the train: the driver's platform is completely different, there are buttons and lights and gauges (as well as a chair) that mean nothing to him (though with a bit of searching, he finds the whistle).
>
> The surgeon cannot operate: the operating theatre is full of high-tech gadgets, monitors, scanners and lasers that appear totally alien. He spends all his time looking for a saw.
>
> The teacher is ready to go after five minutes. All he needed was a code for the photocopier!

It's not a very funny joke, and it doesn't stand up to close scrutiny, but there is an element of truth in it. The fact is that while technology has radically intervened in almost any profession you can think of, the act of teaching has been largely unaffected by these technologies. Little has changed, in effect, since Plato and Aristotle stood on the steps of ancient Athens arguing the toss about democracy. There are those who maintain that teaching is all about the dynamic relationship between tutor and student, and that is why there have been few changes, because this teaching–learning relationship is the central component of education. No e-learning practitioner would disagree with the notion that this dynamic relationship is central to good teaching, yet surely no one is suggesting that I cannot learn anything unless I have a teacher present? I can easily learn many things about many subjects without direct intervention from anyone else. Teaching is essentially about providing a structured, guided and monitored learning experience and there are many ways in which these structures, guides and interactions can be introduced without the teacher being in the same physical space at the same time.

The trouble with FE

Teaching in FE (Further Education) is not without its pressures and few of these are directly related to what goes on in the classroom. As well as being a whizz in the classroom, lecturers are also expected to be able to recite the last three years' Enrolment, Retention and Achievement data for all the courses they teach on, produce great tomes of Self Assessment Reports annually (none of which are ever read by anyone!) and assess increasing amounts of course work for ever-increasing student numbers. In addition, they must also know the Minimum Expected Grade and preferred learning styles of every student they pass in the corridor. At the same time, you'll find them reciting key paragraphs of the *Data Protection Act*, the *Freedom of Information Act*, the *Child Protection Act* and the *Human Rights Act*. Their acute legal minds must also keep abreast of ever changing Health and Safety legislation, and the laws pertaining to racial, sexual and other inequalities. Furthermore, the conscientious lecturer will also keep detailed records of every tutorial and shred any piece of paper with a student's name on it before throwing it away.

And to top all this, you get some bright spark who is a whizz with IT (Information Technology) telling you that you need to transform your teaching and learning activities to encompass a whole raft of new technological developments when you can't even remember your username and password for the college network!

If any of this sounds familiar, then it must be reassuring to realize that you are not alone. It is also true that you, like many of your colleagues, need to be persuaded that ICT (Information and Communications Technology), ILT (Information and Learning Technologies) and e-learning are not only worth the effort, but that they can also genuinely alleviate some of those many other pressures that everyone on the chalk face of education deals with every day.

Not that anyone is suggesting here that e-learning is a panacea for all of FE's ailments, far from it. It is true, however, that certain aspects of ILT can make you (appear at least) more organized, more informed and more prepared for some of the many demands for data placed upon you without you having to shuffle any bits of paper! It is also true that e-learning can rekindle that spark of creativity you had when you first started teaching; when you were prepared to take risks and try new activities; when you were actively learning yourself. You can become reinvigorated and refreshed, even excited at the prospect of teaching; and we all know that the energy and enthusiasm of the teacher is one of the most significant factors in student success (even though it never appears in your Self Assessment Report). Still not convinced?

Arthur C. Clarke is reputed to have described a good idea as having to pass through three stages:

1. It can't be done.
2. It probably can be done, but it isn't worth doing.
3. I knew it was a good idea all along!

When we accept that bringing these new technologies into the classroom is a good idea, then FE as a whole is somewhere between the first and second stages. There is a long way to go yet.

Of course there are the pioneers, the mavericks, the envelope pushers . . . the anoraks. There are those staff who love anything IT and are drawn to gadgets and gizmos, forever tinkering with it and talking about it. I'm not talking necessarily about those staff who teach IT, but there are those who seem genuinely, and worryingly, aroused by the prospect of a software update!

Reasons for avoiding the 'digital revolution'

To help us understand exactly how far FE has to travel on its journey to a digital revolution, we will try identifying and tackling some of the myths and excuses commonly found in the staff and workrooms of FE:

- 'They are trying to replace teachers with computers.'
- 'There is no evidence that using ILT improves learning.'
- 'It is just a fad, and will die out in a couple of years.'
- 'Computers don't like me/I don't get on with computers.'
- 'It can be useful in other subjects, but not mine.'
- 'My students aren't interested in IT.'
- 'I've been teaching for 20 years: I didn't need it then . . .'

They are trying to replace teachers with computers

No one who has taught really believes that computers can replace teachers. There are some non-teaching managers with an eye on the books who might see ILT as a way of saving money by reducing contact time, and in FE the economic pressures are indeed great. A more positive educational reading of the argument, however, is to see that ILT can offer ways of accessing education and learning for groups of people who are unable or unwilling to participate in traditional classroom-based learning. It is our duty to consider all possible avenues of teaching and learning, and not simply hold on to some ancient ideal that the traditional relationship between the tutor and the student is the only possible model of education.

There is no evidence that using ILT improves learning

It is true that there have been some conflicting reports on the success of ILT and e-learning, and this particular debate is likely to rumble on for some time, although there are increasing numbers of reports that suggest there is a clear link between the use of e-learning and improved grades. In the report by the Fischer Family Trust entitled 'Impact of e-learning on GCSE results of 105,617 students, 2004' (SAM Learning 2005) one of the key findings of the report declares that:

Students with over 10 hours use of e-learning achieved 4.7 per cent more 5+ A*–C GCSE grades than expected based on prior attainment. The value added gain was 2.1 capped points per pupil, which is the equivalent of one-quarter of a GCSE grade per subject.

Students engage with learning more positively when it is framed in a context that is familiar. Young people now live in a world in which the Internet, mobile phones and other digital media are the tools by which they negotiate their place in the world. By not including these tools and frameworks in the structures of teaching, we run the risk of increasingly alienating young people from education, making it appear irrelevant and remote from their daily existence.

It is just a fad, and will die out in a couple of years
Every technological development of the last 150 years has had to endure the same arguments. Time will quieten those voices, as they did with air travel, the telephone, television, the motor car, etc.... There is overwhelming evidence that the use of IT will not die out, in fact it has already increased to a point where it has become an integrated part of all developed and developing societies worldwide.

There has been some analysis of numbers using mass communication technology. In *A Brief History of the Future: The Origins of the Internet* (Naughton 2000) there is a dramatic comparison of radio, television and the Internet:

> It took radio 37 years to build an audience of 50 million and television about 15 years to reach the same number of viewers. But it took the World Wide Web *just over three years* to reach *its* first 50 million users!

Also, figures on Internet usage in Great Britain produced by the Office of National Statistics show a steady increase in the numbers who have Internet access at home. The year 2005 was a landmark in as much as Broadband, for the first time, accounted for more than half of all Internet connections in the UK.

Broadband connections continued to increase their market share and made up 52.4 per cent of all subscriptions in June 2005. (Office of National Statistics 2005)

Computers don't like me/I don't get on with computers

Often people who struggle with new technology will invest inanimate objects with a benign or even malevolent personality. These are the very same kind of people who treated the arrival of the photocopier with suspicion and consider the mobile phone to be the principal cause of society's decay. There is a danger that, as the digital revolution finally reaches into the hermetically sealed classroom environment, these staff will become increasingly alienated. These potential digital Luddites need support and encouragement, with much hand-holding and stroking, rather than being dismissed as outdated techno-phobes. More will be said of this later.

It can be useful in other subjects, but not mine

You will frequently find that teachers of vocational subjects can see a relevance for e-learning in academic subjects, and it is also fair to say that academic lecturers see how e-learning could help vocational subjects. The tutor who accepts the general arguments for embracing e-learning, but then sets him/herself aside from the argument as a special case is probably the most difficult convert. They seem reasonable, they seem positive, and almost willing, but don't be fooled. The positive words are a smoke screen designed to send the enthusiastic e-learning practitioner in search of other, more cynical, quarry!

Surely a good teacher would consider how all new developments could be used to improve and enhance the delivery of their subject? No one is proposing that brick layers don't use real muck or that drama students conduct online rehearsals, but there are elements of all subjects that could benefit from the inclusion of e-learning activities, if staff are open-minded in approach.

My students aren't interested in IT

Most students (apart from mathematicians, statisticians and accountants) aren't interested in spreadsheets. Most students aren't interested in databases or doing mail merges with business letters. But this is not really IT, even though it is still the core requirement of Key Skills IT units. If you ask these same students if they would like to learn how to download and manipulate the films, pictures and messages off their mobile phone, or how to set up and publish their own homepages then the response is far more positive. It isn't IT that is the turn off. It is what type of Information and which Technology they are being press-ganged into adopting that causes the indifference. Government research into computer use by young people produced some startling results:

> In autumn 2002, 98 per cent of young people aged 5 to 18 used computers at home, at school or elsewhere – with 22 per cent saying they used computers at school but not at home. For children aged between 11 and 18, the main activities undertaken on a computer at home were school or college work (90 per cent), playing games (70 per cent), and using the Internet (67 per cent). (Office of National Statistics 2002)

If 98 per cent of young people use computers, then how can we possibly argue that 'students don't like IT', unless it is because we are doing something drastically wrong in the delivery of the subject?

I've been teaching for 20 years: I didn't need it then. . .
Despite the fact that almost all young people use computers and own mobile phones, there are those staff who haven't yet recognized that these revolutions are taking place, and believe that the handouts they had in the 1980s serve just as well today. These staff may even have an excellent reputation as teachers, a reputation which was established many years ago when the Internet was just still an idea and mobile phones were as large as house bricks. They have had good relationships with their students, but as their success values start to fall, they will begin blaming the schools, the parents or the students themselves for not being as bright as they used to be, having lower standards, being less able to concentrate, etc. ... We all listen to these words of wisdom, and nod our heads in agreement, 'Yes, that

must be true, because you have always been a good teacher'. The reality is, however, that the world has changed, but the teaching has not.

If the old saying, 'You can't teach an old dog new tricks' is true, then *we* must become *new* dogs! But it is not going to be easy. For example, in one fairly large south-coast college, there is a teacher-training course that offers *one* session on ILT during the whole course! In fact the teacher trainees on this course spend longer learning how to set up and use an OHP (Overhead Projector). To make matters worse, this is delivered in a room with a state-of-the art interactive whiteboard that is more frequently used as a projection surface for the OHP demonstration than for its true purpose!

Life and the Internet

For those who have embraced the digital age, the influence of the Internet on every aspect of our lives has been profound. It is now possible to purchase almost anything over the Internet: cast iron baths, digital cameras, music, holidays. It is also possible to apply for a passport, make a UCAS application, get turned down for a loan and even choose the topping for a large deep pan (or thin and crispy) pizza. If I am a student at a typical FE college and I want to get a copy of an assignment, pick up a handout or check my progress online, then my chances are pretty remote. But why should this be the case? There is not a single argument that will stand up to scrutiny for not offering this kind of service. And if there is no sound argument for not offering this service, and there are compelling educational arguments in favour of such a service, then why should teachers still resist these developments?

Of course there is a significant but minor proportion of the population on the other side of the digital divide: the 22 per cent of young people who don't have access to a computer at home. Once again, the digital Luddite leaps to the defence of the uninitiated, arguing that using ILT puts this group at a significant disadvantage. But the e-learning practitioner will argue that building ILT and e-learning into the core of curriculum activity (along with open access IT facilities) will help break down and eradicate this social barrier by encouraging the development of IT literacy, and providing a greater range of opportunities for future employment. After all, we don't not teach anyone to drive because not everyone owns a car.

Those parts of FE that are reluctant to embrace these emergent technologies are therefore perpetuating the fear of all things IT and reinforcing this digital divide.

Banishing bureaucracy

Walk into any staffroom in any college and ask what the worst thing about the job is and high on the list is 'bureaucracy'. Developments in VLEs and MLEs (Managed Learning Environments) do offer a genuine solution to the admin-weary college lecturers, whose desks are hidden beneath the piles of pro-forma data requests, schemes and quality-review documents (not to mention student assessment portfolios). If you were to enter these same staffrooms with an offer of being able to reduce the level of admin and paperwork and improve efficiency, in exchange for a few hours of training then (apart from the disbelieving howls of laughter) there may well be the chance of a foothold that is so desperately needed. The average PC's (personal computer's) ability to store, organize, analyse and report upon data is quite impressive and with the right data-handling system, you can reduce the need for admin significantly. This will be discussed in more depth in Chapter 6.

Introducing an MIS (Management Information System) into an FE college *can* reduce bureaucracy, but it can also lead to a Kafkaesque explosion of bureaucracy, as this (strange but true) anecdote from an FE manager demonstrates:

> All our Key Skills Registrations have been done centrally for many years. As a manager, I was given the task of compiling KSR forms (Key Skills Registration – if you hadn't guessed) for all the courses I managed. Rather than handwrite them, and to be sure of being accurate, I got the student data (names, dates of birth, etc.) from the MIS report and pasted it into the form to send electronically. To show my keenness, I even used the City & Guilds website to check for students

who already had registration numbers and added their numbers to the list. I emailed them to the exams officer. Two days later, I received my own KSR forms back (someone had printed them out for me) and was told they couldn't be accepted unless they were accompanied by an MIS class list, which I then had to print out, attach to the KSR form and return to the exams officer who would then check the KSR form against the class list, before registering them.

There is more to this tale (including the fact that the exams officer also used the MIS system to enter registration details), but the point is already made. Introducing ILT and e-learning initiatives also requires a change in outlook, a change in activity, a change in behaviour and a change in culture if it is to ever succeed.

So let's move on to take a look at some simple techniques that most teaching staff can use to introduce e-learning into their delivery with very little knowledge of IT or extra effort on their part.

2 Reusing the wheel

As outlined in the previous chapter, a lot of teaching staff in colleges shrink away in horror when they hear the word 'e-learning'. They have an idea in the back of their minds that it is not for them, that it is difficult and time-consuming to produce e-learning materials and that the amount of effort simply is not worth the results produced.

Unfortunately, some colleges have technical support staff who, often inadvertently, manage to promote this myth still further and the whole area becomes the province of 'the expert'. So when should you be using e-learning and when is it simply not worth your time? If it takes significantly longer to prepare your current delivery using e-learning techniques, then maybe you shouldn't be doing it. That's not to say that it isn't worth trying anything new. After all, once a technique is mastered you should be able to use it for many years. But remember that when you are pressed for time, you may be better off with the devil you know than the new one you've just invited in via your computer monitor! It's really a question of devoting some of your available time to developing your e-learning techniques, as it will pay you dividends in the future.

Start off from where you are now, not where you hope you're going to be in six months' time. Can you write a basic Word document? Can you produce a simple PowerPoint presentation? If the answer to the last two questions is 'yes' then you can produce some pretty impressive e-learning delivery without too much time or effort. If the answer is 'no' then you should stop reading and enrol on some staff development programme as soon as possible! In this chapter, I will outline some basic techniques, but remember, you only need to start with one, experiment in using e-learning when you get a little time, then try to integrate it into your normal delivery. Your own experience probably has already shown you that most students are keen to be taught in new and different ways. Most students tend to be very forgiving of mistakes and problems that you might have with equipment – provided they don't keep on happening!

So how many techniques do you really need to know in order to begin integrating e-learning as part of your normal delivery routine and how long will it take to learn them? Those of us who use e-learning as part of our delivery probably all have our favourite techniques, but I think that there are just six basic techniques which will start almost all teaching staff off on the road to delivering e-learning and most of these techniques are to be found in the main office applications that many of us use on a regular basis, i.e. Word and PowerPoint.

My personal list of useful first-time techniques consists of:

- Word comment boxes
- Word drop boxes
- Word Mix and Match
- Word drag and drop using Order
- PowerPoint Form Text Boxes
- PowerPoint sound

Using the half a dozen techniques outlined above, a tutor can add a massive amount of interactivity to their delivery.

Most of us use Word on a regular basis for writing reports and for producing handouts for students but it is surprising how few of us know about using the above techniques to enhance our teaching.

Word

Comment boxes
Comment boxes were designed to allow extra information to be added to a document without changing the actual text on the page. Comments are words which are highlighted as part of a text document and which, when the student points to them with their mouse, open up a little information box just next to the highlighted word. They were originally designed so that

reviewers could make annotations on the screen without changing the document text.

In the older versions of Word, it is as simple as dragging your mouse over a word to highlight it and then using Insert, then Comment to bring up an area that lets you place text into the attached information box. At the bottom of the screen a space appears to allow you to add your comments. Each comment is numbered and if a comment is added by another reviewer then once the learner points at the comment the reviewer's name also appears along with their comment.

This was great and easy to use but in the latest versions of Word the comments now appear as a bubble at the side of the page – one of Bill's 'improvements' that have actually made the technique slightly more complicated for us to use! We can get around this in later versions of Word by selecting Tools > Options > Track Changes and turn off the Balloons option. The comments will appear within square brackets which you can now shade in using the highlighter – a bit tricky for beginners but you only need to do this once!

So how can you use Comments with your students? When might it be useful to add extra text to a document that doesn't show up on-screen until you point at it? Many students find a lot of text on the page is daunting and will respond by either not reading wordy documents at all or by giving up on them after a few sentences. By adding highlighted words using Comments you can increase the content of your on-screen documents without frightening off your learners!

Example of using comment boxes to reduce information overload

One tutor used Comments to explain what the various terms on a financial end-of-year balance sheet meant. She had found that presenting students with a fully detailed balance sheet led to them concentrating on the figures presented rather than on how to actually read the balance sheet itself.

To add an explanation of each individual term led to a page full of information boxes – quite confusing for any learner new to studying accounts! She produced a simplified Word document as shown below which, at first sight, gave the briefest outline of a balance sheet format:

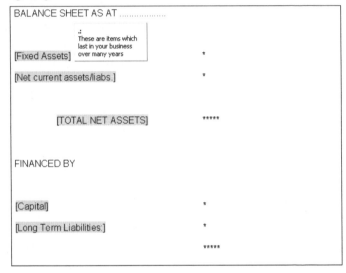

Figure 1

The simplified outline balance sheet above, when presented to the students electronically, allowed them to see a simple overview which, once they pointed their mouse at a particular heading (depicted in square brackets), then revealed a more in-depth explanation of that term as a comment – for example, when a student pointed his/her mouse at 'Fixed Assets' the information: *These are items which last in your business over many years* appeared next to it.

The tutor found that the students began to understand the overall concept of balance sheets much more quickly using this techniques, since they were not presented with a mass of information all at once. She also produced a paper handout for their future reference that included the explanations that had appeared as comments. Since she had already written them out in the comment boxes, the full handout was simple to produce.

This would work for any technical document and can be used to explain in detail what a particular technical word means. Lecturers who have become familiar with using this technique have developed other uses for it such as using Comments to insert Glossaries into their documents.

Another use for Comments is to request your students to undertake additional tasks at certain points in a document.

Example of using Comments to make documents more interactive

One Rural Science tutor specializing in land-based subjects was teaching a group of students from a local school who came in for one afternoon session each week. He decided that to keep their interest over the days between sessions he would set them a series of tasks which he got his technical staff to burn onto a CD for the students to take away and use back at their own school. One example is given below:

GCSE Rural Science
(place the cursor over the yellow box to see the question)

Nutrition: Classification of animals by what they eat

When we look at animals and what they eat there are three distinct groups. These are:

> .:
> Write in the space below 3 animals of this type

1. Herbivores These are animals that eat only plants.

a.

b.

c.

2. Carnivores These are animals that eat only other animals.

Figure 2

The students were also provided with a paper copy of the document above with added instructions as to which file it related to and where to find it on their CD. When they opened up the document and pointed the mouse at the word 'Herbivore' an instruction appeared: '*Write in the space below 3 animals of this type*'. The students then wrote their answers down on the sheet and brought it into the college the following week so that it could be handed to their peers to enable it to be marked in the group and the various answers could be discussed within the session. They really took to this way of studying and some even took the CDs home so that they could use them on their own computers.

The above is a simple example of how a little thought can enable us to add a basic form of interactivity to a learning activity. The creation of simple exercises such as this for use either online or via a CD is not technically very difficult and is certainly not beyond most staff in FE. As we have seen, the results can be used to demonstrate understanding of the subject and can be included in further group discussions and exercises.

A third major way in which Comments can be used is to actually comment directly on a student's work. This only works if students provide their assessments in the form of Word documents, but it can be very effective as you can highlight sections of their document and add comments on their work in the context of their actual submission.

Comments also have the ability to include sound recordings and you could also use this facility to add verbal comments to a document if you wish. If you are a Harry Potter fan, then you will have heard of Ron Weasley opening up a 'howler' from his mother and being shouted at directly from the letter! You could do exactly the same with a verbal comment and offer very concise and direct advice on your students' work within the actual documents! It is also possible to use this technique to enable students to record explanations of work that they have undertaken. For example, if they are on a design course, they could actually include a discussion on the images that they have included.

The above examples illustrate that even when using a very simple technique – such as Comments, a simple facility within Word – you can open up a wide range of interactive e-learning-based tasks that can add variety to your learners' experience. As tutors it is up to us to use our skills and experience to develop such facilities into effective learning tools for our students.

Drop boxes

Drop boxes are another facility of Word. They allow the student to choose from a selection of options from a list that drops down from where the mouse is clicked within a text document. They use the powerful Forms feature in Word that can be found under View > Toolbars > Forms.

First, type out a space in your text and place your cursor in the middle of it. From the Forms toolbar choose Drop Down Form Field to add the drop box, then Form Field Options to put in your alternative answers. Once done, click on Protect Form and the next time a student points to the box with their mouse a drop-down list will appear.

You can use drop boxes to place a multiple-choice box anywhere in your text document where you have left blank space and they can be used to test understanding of terms used in a particular subject by allowing the student to select the correct word from a list to fill this space.

At its simplest level, a few basic words can be placed in a brief description and the student must then choose the correct one. For example, the sentence 'Income tax is collected by . . .' could have the words 'Local Authorities' or 'HM Revenue and Customs' as two options and the student then selects the correct option. The student can then print out the description with his/her answer to allow it to be assessed.

However, drop boxes can be used in other ways; the same list of words can be placed at different places in a piece of text and the most appropriate choices can be selected in turn until the entire list of words has been used up.

Example of using drop boxes to make documents more 'interactive'

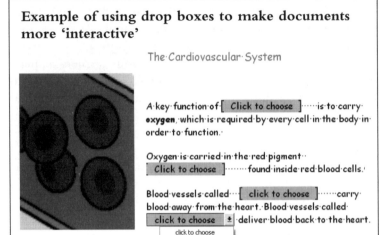

The Cardiovascular System

A key function of [Click to choose] ⋯is to carry oxygen, which is required by every cell in the body in order to function.

Oxygen is carried in the red pigment ⋯ [Click to choose] ⋯⋯found inside red blood cells.

Blood vessels called⋯ [click to choose] ⋯⋯carry blood away from the heart. Blood vessels called [click to choose ⋄] deliver blood back to the heart.

| click to choose |
| arteries |
| veins |

Figure 3

The above example uses the same list of words in the final two drop boxes. The student has to choose which word is most appropriate at each point in the paragraph. One advantage of this technique is that the tutor can easily copy the list to as many different parts of the document as they wish.

This technique can also be used with images. A series of blank lines is placed onto a page. This is necessary since drop boxes can only be placed in the page text itself. An image is then inserted onto the page. The choices for the various parts of the image are then placed into a form and the drop box is copied down the page, once for each choice that is available. A line is then drawn from each drop box to the separate parts of the image and the image labelling exercise is complete.

Mix and Match

Word Mix and Match uses the text-box facility that is part of the drawing tools. The text boxes that you create with this function can be moved around on a page by using the mouse to drag and drop each box.

You could use Mix and Match to get students to label an image. A series of text boxes containing the label headings is placed onto the page in a random order and the student is asked to drag and drop them onto the image in the appropriate place. One sports tutor has used this technique to develop students' understanding of leg muscle structure by asking them to place muscle names next to the appropriate muscle. You can also use this technique to move text boxes containing certain terms to match them up with a particular explanation.

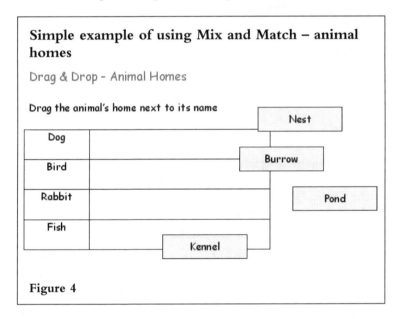

Simple example of using Mix and Match – animal homes

Drag & Drop – Animal Homes

Drag the animal's home next to its name

Dog	Nest
Bird	Burrow
Rabbit	Pond
Fish	
	Kennel

Figure 4

Drag and drop using Order

You can use 'drag and drop' in many different ways. One of the easiest and most useful is to enable the student to select correct and incorrect options by using the Order facility.

This facility, which is available when you right click on a drawn object or image, allows you to place text boxes, rectangles or images into different orders on a page, e.g. on top of other items, behind other items or in between other items, a bit like shuffling cards.

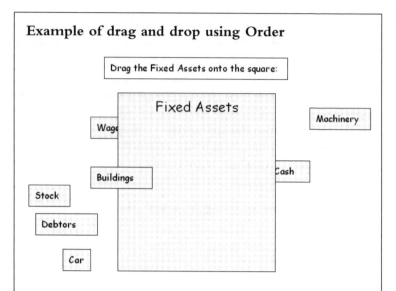

Example of drag and drop using Order

Drag the Fixed Assets onto the square:

Fixed Assets

Machinery

Wage

Buildings

Cash

Stock

Debtors

Car

Figure 5

The students dragged the items onto the central square. Incorrect items were 'sent to the back' of the square using the Order feature so that they would appear to be behind the square, correct items were 'brought to the front' of the square to appear on top of the square.

The teacher used this technique with students to reinforce the idea of 'fixed' and 'current' assets. If the learner had got it wrong, the item simply seemed to disappear from the page!

Again, this is a very simple and easy-to-learn technique, but one which can have many uses in the learning environment once you are aware that it is there.

PowerPoint

PowerPoint is probably one of the most used examples of presentation software in education. When tutors think of e-learning, many of them tend to think it starts and ends with PowerPoint. Once they have placed their old overhead transparencies onto a PowerPoint presentation, then they feel that they have converted their materials into 'e-learning'. Unfortunately, this is not actually the case. E-learning is much more than colourful (or not so colourful) PowerPoint slides which, apart from being available as a file instead of on a transparent sheet, are basically the same as those that have been used for decades in most learning organizations. Of course, there is nothing wrong with PowerPoint in itself, and done well, as part of an enthusiastic and encouraging learning session, it can have a massive impact. Unfortunately, there is still a tendency amongst many tutors to cause the famous 'death by Power-Point' which goes on in many sessions.

It's a shame, really, since PowerPoint can be so much more than a convenient way of rattling off a series of electronic slides. It has many features which, whilst they might take a short while to work out, can enhance a presentation and bring interactivity into almost all learning sessions.

Once again, we don't need to understand in-depth techniques to get a lot more out of PowerPoint than many tutors currently do. We shall look at just two enhancements to PowerPoint which are relatively easy to produce, but can add interactivity to your sessions – Text Boxes within Forms and recording and using sound.

Form Text Boxes
This is still a relatively unusual way of using PowerPoint and can be done without too much difficulty. Using Form Text Boxes in PowerPoint can allow you to record student responses directly onto your slides and enable you, and your students, to review them at a later time. In other words it can act like an electronic flipchart!

Before you start, it's best to set your slide background to a darker colour, as the text box is set to be white as standard and so does not stand out too well on a blank page! Once this is done, select View > Toolbars > Control Toolbox. A graphic menu appears which shows several options that we are already familiar with from the Word Forms menu. Choose the Text

Box. Once you have done this, you can draw a rectangle onto your slide into which you can place text. Unfortunately, the standard setting on PowerPoint means that once you start typing, the text doesn't wrap onto the next line. This can be a real pain when you are entering ideas from students as, once you have got to the end of the first line in the text box, it begins to slide off to the left and the start of your line disappears!

To get around this problem, you can either make sure that the students' replies are fairly short, or you can right click in the text box and select Properties from the drop-down menu that appears. A seemingly horrendous list of options is shown, but don't worry, we only want to change one of them! They are shown in two columns, the title followed by the setting, and just over halfway down the list is the option Multiline. Click at the word False next to it and a drop box appears, click on this and select True. From now on, your text should drop to the next line once you get to the right of the text box.

The really useful bit, from an e-learning point of view, is that whatever is in the text box when you end the slideshow is retained in the box. This means that you can save it and use it again, either in following sessions, or by printing it out for student notes, or for placing somewhere that all your students can access electronically. How you might use it again is up to you, but already you have begun to use PowerPoint as something more than a glorified overhead projector!

Example using PowerPoint text boxes
One tutor used this technique for recording ideas from buzz groups and used the thoughts saved within the PowerPoint presentation to recap with the students at the start of their next session.

He used one PowerPoint slide at the end of a session to record their thoughts on what e-learning consisted of:

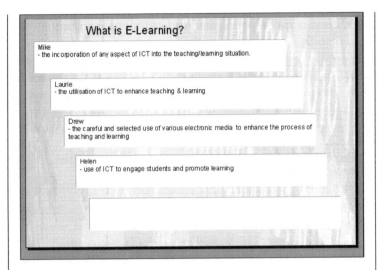

Figure 6

At the start of the next session, he reopened this slide and used this as the basis for developing ideas within the next session.

A useful tip with this technique is not to enter more than five large blocks of text, as the students can become bored if the process takes more than a few minutes. Remember, just because you are providing learning in an electronic format, the rules for learning situations still apply. Use the same technique for too long or too often, and your audience will quickly become bored.

Sound

Sound clips can be a powerful tool for sessions such as ESOL (English for Speakers of Other Languages) teaching, or to overcome certain accessibility problems. To record sound is relatively simple, but, once again, it is a facility that not many tutors get around to using. In PowerPoint, you use Insert > Movies and sound > Record sound (you do need to have a microphone handy!). Click on the red circular Record button that appears on the screen and, once you finish, click on the square blue Stop button. The sound recording is dropped onto the slide you are preparing and you can move it around in your presentation just like an image.

You can also insert sounds from other sources if you wish, which leads to the possibility of students being able to record their own sound clips and incorporating them into a presentation.

Example of bringing sound into a PowerPoint presentation

One tutor used sounds in conjunction with text boxes as described above to produce simple exercises which asked students to spell certain words. To do this using a standard text-based question would not be possible, since the question would have included the correct spelling of the word itself!

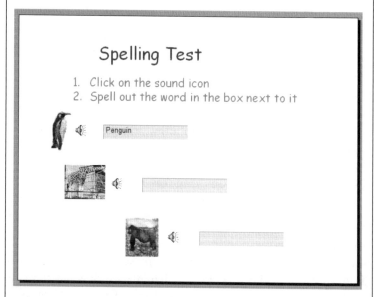

Figure 7

When the student clicked on the sound icon, they were asked to spell a certain word e.g. 'Please spell penguin'. The students entered their attempts and once the set of slides was complete they saved the PowerPoint presentation. Since the text boxes also saved the spellings that they attempted, the tutor could assess each individual student's progress.

Using just these two simple examples, the tutor can begin to move PowerPoint away from its meagre existence as a glorified overhead projector!

And, so far, we haven't strayed from the main applications within the Microsoft Office suite, most of which we use on a regular basis to prepare our handouts!

I would recommend that you get familiar with the techniques above. They really do require very little background knowledge and can be used to great effect to add interactivity to your presentations and to your students' learning.

A bit further down the line

Excel can also be an effective e-learning tool, but the interactivity is a bit trickier to develop. With a little knowledge you can not only use drop boxes such as those outlined in the section on Word, but also you can get the spreadsheets to mark student replies and provide feedback in interactive quizzes! Once you have mastered the six techniques outlined above, seek out your e-learning development person to see how you can extend your ideas into Excel.

You can add even more interactivity by using other features of Office; you could, for example, use the Hyperlinks options in Word to allow your online handouts to become non-linear, i.e. you can link certain words or sections of text to parts of other documents or even to relevant pages on the Internet. Once you start experimenting with hyperlinking it's amazing how quickly you start looking at broadening out your presentations. Why not, for example, have links to different levels of text to allow for differentiated learning within a particular group, or link to different levels of questions for different students?

You can even use PowerPoint in a non-linear way and move on to certain slides depending on the response to the initial slide. This feature allowed one tutor to use hyperlinks that were attached to a set of answer buttons next to a set of questions. She had produced an interactive quiz which, when the wrong button was clicked, took the student to a 'whoops – incorrect' page, and, if they clicked on the correct button, it moved them on to the next question in the quiz.

 Remember, you don't have to keep reinventing the wheel – once you have an interactive piece of work that you find is useful with your students, then you can save it and simply change parts of it to produce entirely new mix-and-match questions, new PowerPoint quizzes and a host of other materials.

Once you have mastered this intermediate stage, then you could even use the formulas featured in Excel to produce those interactive quizzes mentioned earlier which provide feedback for the students on screen that varies depending on what answer the student selected from a drop box.

A little initial effort in experimenting with these techniques can result in saving you a lot of time in the long term. Remember, you are not alone – many other lecturers are busy producing examples which you can use as a basis for your own interactive techniques and, provided you know which bits to change, you may not even need to know how to set up a similar example from scratch. The Ferl site at ferl.becta.org.uk is an example of a site that has lots of useful examples that you can download.

A little more knowledge of the Background options on the Office suite of programs can take you a long way towards producing a host of interesting and interactive materials in your sessions.

3 Death by PowerPoint

Alternative programs that you might like to use

In the previous chapter we mentioned how you could use simple techniques to make PowerPoint into a useful tool for e-learning. PowerPoint itself has been around for years – the idea of producing overhead transparencies which can incorporate images relatively effortlessly and which can be changed in moments along with text that can be animated, and, best of all, updated before each new session is certainly a winner.

PowerPoint is now a standard part of most tutors' basic presentation techniques. It is being used everywhere; in many cases, it is being misused as well. Most of us can remember sitting through a pretty dire PowerPoint presentation at some time or other and wishing that the presenter had used just a little bit more imagination. Slide after slide of black and white lines of text, often with the entire slide being presented to the audience at once and in font sizes that require you to use a set of opera glasses to read them properly, can all too often be seen at conferences and training events. It is often the case that a large chunk of the audience are not taking in the subject of the presentation but wondering how long there is before the next coffee break!

So why should we imagine that it is any different for our students? They have PowerPoint thrust at them in nearly every room where the facility is available and often it is used to present information in much the same way that OHPs were used over 30 years ago. Increasingly, the students have come from a school background where PowerPoint and interactive whiteboards are regularly used and the 'wow' factor that used to carry many presentations through has largely gone. In many cases, the students themselves can often produce presentations that are as good as, or even better than, those presented by the tutor. Perhaps it is time to give PowerPoint a rest and come up with some alternative ways of getting information and ideas across in a teaching session?

In this chapter we shall be taking a look at some other readily available programs that can be put to good use by tutors. None of them are costly (some are free), and they are all designed to be easy to use. They include:

Hot Potatoes
Action Mazes
Mind Mapping
Content Management Tools
WebQuests

The above list is by no means comprehensive, but it provides the relative newcomer to e-learning with a range of alternatives to PowerPoint presentations.

Hot Potatoes

Hot Potatoes is a very popular piece of software that is used throughout all levels of education and is produced by Half-Baked Software, Inc. It allows you to make simple interactive exercises that are presented to the student as Web-based pages and can therefore be used either at a distance from your college or organization over the Web, or via a college Intranet (Internal Net). They have even been used on the small handheld computers known as PDAs (Personal Digital Assistants).

The program allows you to make five different types of exercises that you set up using basic templates. Once you have done this, you simply save your work and the program converts your exercises into a Web format automatically. The exercises can also be linked together, a useful feature which allows you to take the student through a series of different tasks. Another useful feature is that the pages can be set up to provide clues for the students which give them the ability to correct any mistakes they might make and tutors can also enter their own answer –

in other words, to provide specific feedback which allows the student to reflect on any incorrect answers given.

Hot Potatoes scores the student based on the replies that he/she gives and these can also be emailed to the tutor to allow tracking of student progress.

The five types of Hot Potatoes exercises are:

- Jquiz – This allows you to produce question-based exercises.
- Jmix – A jumbled-word exercise in which the student arranges jumbled-up words into phrases or sentences.
- Jcross – A crossword puzzle creator.
- Jcloze – A fill-in-the-blank exercise where the student enters the words that are missing.
- Jmatch – A matching exercise where the student matches items in one column with those in another.

Jquiz
This can produce four types of question:

- Multiple-choice questions that allow the student to click on a series of buttons and to get feedback on the choices made.
- Multi-selection questions that can have several correct answers: the student gets feedback when all their choices have been made.
- Short-answer questions that allow the student to type their own answer into a box.
- Hybrid questions that start off as short answer and change to multiple-choice if the student doesn't get them right in two attempts.

Jmix
This exercise works both with entire words and with individual letters and allows the student to click on his/her choices in turn or to drag things into their correct places.

Jcross
This is a simple crossword maker, best used for beginners with the Automatic Grid Maker that can be found in the Manage

Grid option. Using this option, all you have to do is type each word in, then click the Make the Grid button and the crossword is generated for you using all the words that it can fit in. Put a title on your crossword and type in the clues and you are ready to go!

Jcloze

The students fill in gaps in a text document that have been set by the tutor. They click on a Check button to see which they have got right and are scored on how many correct answers they have given.

Jmatch

This can include images as well as text and items can be matched by choosing from drop-down boxes or by dragging and dropping items together.

Added Extras

There are several useful extras that can be included in all the various types of Hot Potatoes exercises above. A piece of text can be added to the page and a timer can be set so that students only have a set period of time to complete their tasks.

Once you have completed each quiz, the program converts it into a Web-ready format so that you could then place it onto your Intranet. You can even link several types of quizzes together using The Masher but this is slightly more complicated for the beginner. Hot Potatoes is distributed as shareware and, provided that you are working in a non-profit-making state-funded educational institution and you place all materials made using the software onto a public website where everyone can use them freely, then you can use Hot Potatoes free of charge.

Action Mazes

One of the things that the Web is very good at is linking backwards and forwards through pages that provide a string of possibilities. However, it can be difficult for tutors to take advantage of this facility effectively with students. One way to do this is to use Action Mazes.

An Action Maze is based on simple adventure stories and

enables the student to progress from page to page based on the decisions that he/she has made previously.

Students are given a scenario and have to make a choice which takes them on to the next phase of the story. Action Mazes can be used to good effect when looking at areas such as equal opportunities or discrimination, where the results of choices made can have important repercussions.

You will need to plan carefully beforehand for what problems and choices you want to present the student with. A sketched-out flow diagram is often best, with each option mapped out to the next scenario. Mind maps, mentioned in the next section, can be used to good effect here.

Quandary, also produced by Half-Baked Software, Inc. allows you to develop Action Maze exercises quickly. You might want to use them for simple procedural examples. An example of this is to assess what a student would do if he/she saw an accident – the student is presented with a series of situations and has to make the best decision based on the choices put to him/her. Each choice made then either outlines the consequences of a selected action upon the casualty if it is wrong, or moves on to the next stage if it is right. The whole exercise has a built-in timer and the student gets four minutes to make the choices in the right order and save the life of the casualty.

Simple Action Mazes can be used in a lot of ways with a little imagination and are relatively easy to construct.

Mind Mapping

This software can be used to produce mind maps which organize tasks and information in a very visual format. The program was originally designed to organize ideas and plans but it can also be used to generate projects and essays. Words can be overlaid on images, as can numbers and colour coding, that help the visual learner to take in information in a simpler way.

Begin with an image in the centre of your screen and add key words and images which fan out from this central image. These words and images are connected to the centre via lines, and lines also connect them to further images or words which derive from, and relate to, topics and ideas that stem from that line of thought. Images, symbols, codes and outlines can highlight specific areas of the map and help to keep the students' interest. Because a mind map is visual it can help visual learners to make linkages between ideas more quickly. It allows both the tutor and the students to concentrate on thoughts and ideas much more clearly and concisely.

As well as using Mind Mapping software to plan activities, it is very useful for communicating, presenting and organizing information and ideas. You can use mind maps to take notes in brain-storming sessions and for summarizing and making overviews of your course or a single lecture. Many Mind-Mapping programs have the ability to generate the mind maps as Web pages, Word documents or PowerPoint presentations.

One useful tip with mind maps is to use colours to differentiate areas and help to give added meaning to sections of the map. Both the text itself and the background can normally be colour-coded and can add an extra dimension to the line of thought. If nothing else colour can allow a thread to be followed easily.

One tutor wanted a way to quickly link to the e-learning materials produced by the National Learning Network (NLN). Since there was a vast amount of materials to link to, he used a mind map to organize his links. With nearly 20 general topic areas and over 1,600 modules, the breadth of materials that they provide can often be overwhelming when you want to use them in a session.

The tutor linked several mind maps together using hyperlinks so that the overall topic areas were displayed on the first mind map and when a topic such as science was clicked on the various subject areas within were then displayed on another mind map. He could then keep drilling down through the various layers until he found the module that he wished to use with the students in the session. True, this could have been done as a database, but the specific tutor found this a much easier way of getting to the module he required very quickly. Mind maps are very easy to set up and, as illustrated above, can be put to many different uses in education.

Content management tools

Content management tools can be used by tutors to pick and mix from the e-learning content that is available to them, for instance, the massive range of NLN e-learning modules mentioned above, and to take them apart and link them in with their own, or their colleagues', organization-specific content. These tools can also enable tutors to quickly and easily convert their Word or PowerPoint materials into a format that either links with VLEs or can be published on the Web. Many interactive features can also be added at this stage. There is a wide range of content management tools available but the most popular ones in the UK are listed below.

Acce-lerator

This tool uses a Web-based method that allows you to reuse and to repurpose your materials. Instead of the software sitting on your desktop, it links directly to the Web and is therefore an online tool. As you select your learning objects, they are stored on a central computer. You create your course materials and once you are happy with the results Acce-lerator packs them together in a compressed file called a 'zip' file and sends them down the Web to your desktop. You then uncompress them from this file and use them directly from your computer or from your Intranet. You can even store and use the materials from a CD. They will also work in VLEs.

The advantage of storing the materials centrally on the Web is that they can be shared not just within your own organization but also with other institutions.

Acce-lerator is available at www.acce-lerator.net

CourseGenie, ecat and e-learning objects

All these programs make use of a 'plug-in' to Word – this means that they use the ready-made facilities within Word to enable it to convert documents for you.

These particular programs use plug-ins that can help you to set up Web-based courses easily. They do this by taking your Word documents and allowing you to easily convert these to HTML (Hypertext Markup Language) (Web) documents. This is not the same as the Save as a Web Page option, as the plug-in allows you to perform a lot of other actions, for example you can split your document up into separate pages and add interactivity in the form of various quizzes.

The advantage of this type of software is that you don't have to learn anything about HTML or writing Web pages, you simply take your current Word documents and process them via the plug-in. This allows non-technical staff (most of us) to produce a lot of Web-based materials in a short space of time without having to learn new technical skills.

CourseGenie is very popular in Adult and Community Learning since it can add various types of quizzes and produces nice-looking output. Its most important aspect is that it sits within MS Word and is really easy for tutors to learn to use.

In addition, it is fully accessible for SENDA (*Special Educational Needs and Disabilities Act*), and because it is based on using Styles – short pieces of programming that tell Word exactly how it should be looking on the screen – it is excellent in terms of accessibility. Using Styles means that visually impaired learners can screen-read the outline view of a document and go straight to the section they want to use, as the 'look' of the screen can be changed very easily.

 CourseGenie is available at www.horizonwimba.com

ecat is another form of Word plug-in that allows you to produce Web-ready content directly from a Word document. However, it has one more trick up its sleeve as it can also link via the Web to a central storage computer that can then hold the converted files and catalogue them using a standard method of categorizing data called 'metatagging'. Metatagging is another term for adding a set of descriptions about your learning materials that can be sorted and searched. Any item placed on to this central computer or 'repository' is then available for tutors in other organizations to use.

Lectora, Seminar and Trainersoft are other author tools which all come on a CD. They use a range of preconfigured templates and you can include text images and animations on your pages. They also allow you to add a range of quizzes and assessments to your Web pages, the results from which can be integrated into a range of VLEs.

As can be seen from progams such as ecat, there is

increasingly a move to allow you as tutors to reuse materials that have been produced by e-learning companies or by members of staff from your own or other organizations. It would also be useful to be able to repurpose the materials that are becoming available to us. It may be that an e-learning module is just too large for you to use with your students in the way that you want to and that only one section is actually relevant to the way in which you deliver to your particular students. It may also be that materials have been produced for delivery using one particular type of VLE and so need 'breaking apart' before they are actually useful to you.

There is a move to break down e-learning and other materials into their component parts (termed 'learning objects'). Once this has been done, the idea is that it should then be fairly simple for you as a tutor to find a specific learning object, or set of learning objects, and edit them according to how you deliver your courses. Tutors have always been skilful at reusing materials with different groups of students and in repurposing their materials for different courses. Simply altering the complexity of a task but using the same basic learning material can save a lot of time.

> Any set of digital assets has a number of potential content objects to build into differing learning objects. A two-minute film clip of troops in trenches in the First World War, for example, could be appropriately contextualised to support elements of GCSE History, A level Sociology, a degree in Psychology or a post-graduate programme in Media Studies.
> 'Learning objects under the spotlight',
> Bob Powell, Ferl, 2003

Once materials have been broken down into their component parts, then there are programs available which allow you to stitch the parts back together in ways specifically of benefit to your students.

Reload
Reload is a program that packages up learning objects by storing and indexing them for you in tailor-made sessions. These learning objects can come from various other programs

such as NLN units, PowerPoint presentations, Hot Potatoes quizzes, Excel simulations, video clips as well as Word documents. Reload allows them all to be sorted according to how the tutor wants to have them displayed for the student. They can then be used as part of a presentation for a lecture or workshop, or by the students independently over the Web or an Intranet. The result will also link directly into your VLE. The content is stored on your own desktop and so can fairly readily be altered by you to suit the needs of other students.

@ More details are available at www.reload.ac.uk

WebQuests

WebQuests was first developed by Bernie Dodge from San Diego State University in 1995. The student is directed to a series of websites and has the task of looking up information from each site. The tricky bit is to try to get the student to do more than simply search sites and recall the information. He/she has to make some sort of evaluation and/or appraisal of the information that they obtain from the sites.

The Web quest is usually presented to the students on paper and consists of a series of tasks. Increasingly, the tasks are also made available online through a VLE or Intranet. The students can then work through the tasks individually or in small groups and discuss the results obtained. This technique can also be used to encourage self-study by individual students.

Web quests are really a way of making the best use of a student's time on the Internet. Just allowing students to surf the Net without a clear task in mind when there are now billions of Web pages available can lead to a lot of wasted time!

Most Web quests have the following structure:

- an introduction that contains relevant background to the quest;
- a set of tasks that the student can readily achieve in the available time and which are structured to keep their interest;
- a set of information with pointers to specific websites or pages;

- guidance on how to use the information from the websites visited;
- a 'closing point' to the quest that also outlines what the student has learnt and where they might go to find out more.

The quest can also link in to online assistance from tutors if needed and is a good way of developing a student's ideas and information–gathering skills.

As you can see from the number of tools outlined in this chapter, there is a whole range of alternative programs for use by tutors that don't look anything like PowerPoint. Try one or two of them in your own sessions and your students will really appreciate it, but remember *why* you are using them. If your session hasn't been designed with teaching and learning in mind in the first place, it doesn't matter what you choose, it still won't be effective!

So much for the software – we can go a long way down the e-learning road with what we have already got but what about the nuts and bolts? The next chapter takes a look at what kind of equipment we might want to use as part of our e-learning delivery.

4 Inside the digital classroom

The digital revolution

There isn't a consumer device going that hasn't had some sort of digital overhaul, and as a parlour game you could try and list them all. For extra points, you could point out that the first such overhaul was the digital watch, back in 1972; you may be old enough to remember those clunky red LEDs that were activated by pressing a button on the side.

It is no surprise, then, that the tools and resources we may use in teaching and learning should, eventually, also be given this digital overhaul, even if it is getting on for 40 years since the process started with the wristwatch. Obviously, the computer (PC or Mac) is at the heart of this transformation, and all the other resources are interwoven with this central resource: digital cameras, scanners, webcams, iPods, mobile phones, PDAs and other devices. New terms are introduced to entice us into trying out the technology: external devices are 'plug and play' and some are even 'hot pluggable'.

Let us henceforth refer to our computer not as a PC, but as a 'digital hub'; the centrepiece in a sophisticated array of technologies which converge seamlessly in a teaching and learning environment.

Computers can finally do all those things they had always promised, and much more besides. We are not interested here in computer power, clock speed or any figure that is meaningless to us (other than as a point of comparison). It is the practical application of the technology, the *creative* possibilities that the newer machines can offer: video editing and image manipulation, sound recording and music creation, interactive learning and content creation. Consider also that the software capabilities of a few years ago, which were only ever available to successful creative professionals, are now bundled free with every computer. Not only this, but from a cost point of view, it is now practically cheaper to create a college-wide wireless network than it is to install a cable-based infrastructure and the cost of every other peripheral has also fallen significantly.

Less than a generation ago, it would have taken an investment of tens of thousands of pounds, as well as a massively expensive, top-of-the-range computer, to creatively equip an individual with these tools. Now, for under a thousand pounds, you can walk out of a high-street shop with the entire kit, including a computer with DVD burner, scanner, printer, digital stills camera, digital video camera, microphone, headphones and a musical keyboard, complete with all the software you need to get you started!

These then are the resources of the digital classroom, and with the addition of a few other bits of kit, your average FE tutor could be transformed into a creative learning entrepreneur, working at the cutting edge of the e-learning strategy! Let us consider some of the potential inherent in these developments.

Make it snappy

A good-quality stills camera is the most cost effective way of introducing digital creativity into the classroom. If you can take a picture and have it instantly relayed and displayed to a group for no expense whatsoever, then, with a little creative application, you can enhance those most difficult of topics. And here is a tip: use it primarily with those classes and topics that traditionally seem hardest to teach. Think creatively and take a risk: you will have little to lose in these circumstances and you may just find a way in to a difficult subject.

The first suggestion frequently made by staff when given a camera is simply to record the process and the outcome. The camera is used as an alternative, or in conjunction with, the written record. Examples include scientific experiments, construction processes and rehearsals. This is, of itself, a significant step and an acknowledgement that the introduction of technology can enhance and support curriculum activity, although it isn't exactly creative.

Once tutors become familiar with the concept of digital stills in the classroom, we begin to see the emergence of creativity in teaching and learning exercises.

Here are a few examples:

1. *Teaching IT to drama students*
   It is never going to be easy, but one IT tutor came up with the idea of putting together actors' CVs using a digital stills camera. She took their pictures, uploaded them all onto the VLE along with a template and suddenly she got the attention of an otherwise unruly bunch of *prima donnas*. This was all done in a single session!

2. *French oral*
   The French tutor could see that he and his students were becoming jaded by the same old pictures and exercises. He handed out a couple of cameras and gave the group the task of creating a photo story. These images were dropped into a slide show and projected onto the whiteboard and *voilà*! The resulting improvised dialogues kept the students entertained and engaged for the next few sessions.

3. *Biology*
   To help with experiments in observing plant growth in varying conditions, the students came and took pictures in the lab twice a day for a half term. The resulting stills were then dropped into QuickTime and converted into an animated sequence.

Now hear this

MP3 is the digital standard for audio, and like photography, once the cost of consumable materials is eradicated through the digitalization of the process (no tapes, mixing desks or additional equipment are necessary) then an initial modest investment can pay dividends in the hands of creative teachers. Recording presentations and lectures to enable students to access them through the Internet is one possibility. With a little technical know-how, or the support of someone else, it is relatively easy to record a lecture and convert it to a modest downloadable file, and if you call it a 'Revision Podcast' you will suddenly be considered an innovative e-learning practitioner! But this only scratches the surface of what is possible with audio.

Another sound application of audio (excuse the pun) is to encourage students with literacy issues to create audio diaries for major projects. This has been possible for a long time with some awards such as BTEC (Business and Technology Education Council), but the practical restrictions of the old technology had generally been a disincentive. This is no longer the case. Give your student a recordable MP3 player, which can be bought easily using petty cash and they'll be able to ramble on forever. They can then easily edit these files on a PC or Mac before submission. No complex or expensive technical equipment is needed, nor indeed is a great deal of technical know-how.

Video: on demand

The ease with which high-quality video can be digitized, edited and burnt onto DVD has ceased to impress anyone other than those who remember the first VHS players in schools which needed the weight of a large child to help press down the play button. You can imagine here that I am going to encourage staff to start picking up camcorders and making lots of educational films; after all, anyone can do it, can't they? Not quite. I've seen many such projects made by well-meaning tutors and they are generally pretty awful. In reality, any fool can pick up and point a camera, but you can usually tell within the first few seconds of the resulting film that they are not 'film-makers'. Films made by tutors without proper training tend to look like the endless holiday footage your uncle makes you sit through, except it doesn't have any sea, sand or smiling people. No consideration is given to the lighting and there is a tendency to have lots of camera action: zooming in and out, panning to the left and right, up and down, not able to stop fiddling with the settings. In one shot, everyone will look orange, in the next a pale sickly blue. You would never offer your car keys to someone who fancied themselves as a driver and say 'Off you go ... you'll pick it up as you go' so why expect untrained tutors to produce professional films?

The most useful tip for tutors who want to make their own masterclass videos is 'Leave it to the experts': your students have been watching professionally produced TV programmes and films for many years and have high expectations and a discerning eye for poor quality.

If you do want to make your own videos, then make sure you get the assistance of someone who knows what they are doing. Free yourself from the technical worries and concentrate on the content. If you have the support (or are a naturally gifted film director) then self-generated video materials can provide a focused and outcome-specific resource that will last for many years.

So much for making educational videos, but again this is only the tip of the digital iceberg. What if it is the *students* who have regular and easy access to the camcorder and editing software. Video diaries? Obviously. Recorded presentations for Key Skills portfolios? Of course. But what about getting the students to create their own time-lapse videos of cloud formation or cell growth? In psychology or biology, you could explore involuntary reflexes of the iris to a series of given stimuli (you remember *Bladerunner* don't you?). Almost any observable activity can be reinterpreted and redefined by creative application of an increasingly inexpensive resource. This controlled use of digital video is much easier to manage educationally than the production of educational epics. The resource is tied to specific activities and objectives and as a result is likely to be more successful.

Swimming upstream

Before we abandon the topic of video, let us consider how emergent technologies are offering new possibilities worthy of consideration. The expansion of network infrastructures and the ability to stream media files over an Intranet allows for further educational applications. The current copyright legislation permits educational institutions to digitize any off-air recordings and store them on a network server. This enables, for example, groups of students to use college PCs to access radio and TV broadcasts separately and/or simultaneously. These netcasts, or streaming media files, can be fed into a classroom at specified times, or be available for on-demand downloads. Rather than show a video in the class, you can instruct students to access the stream or use a video-on-demand service as part of their preparation for the next class without having to worry about multiple VHS copies or circulating a single DVD around the group. But you could go further. If your video footage is stored on a streaming-enabled server you can create a tiny link file that will point to this stored media and start playing it instantly. This means that if you use a USB memory stick, or even a floppy disk (no one still uses them do they?), you can carry around this tiny link or hook file; in essence you are carrying around a TV station in your back pocket! Another possibility is to email this link file to a group of students who will all be able to access your prepared footage instantly.

Why WiFi?

Once colleges have embraced the notion that wireless networks are cheaper, easier to maintain, more flexible and just as secure as a cable infrastructure, then we will also see a shift in how laptops, PDAs and tablet PCs are used in the classroom. For example, in a film studies class, the tutor hands out a bundle of wireless tablet PCs from a trolley and introduces an active research project. In small groups, students explore the life, works and critiques of an influential film director on the Internet. When the time comes to feedback their findings, the tutor has the ability to share each screen across the whole class. Charts and diagrams can be drawn, shared and printed with ease and at the end of the class the tablet PCs are returned to the trolley and recharged. There is no need to book a PC lab and drag a class across the college into a room where the tutor spends the next hour staring at the back of the students' heads. The activity takes place in the students' usual environment and the technology is no more obtrusive than using large textbooks.

Multi-tasking multi-skilled multi-media

Some very user-friendly editing software, such as iMovie for Mac, allows you to be far more flexible and creative than the film-making scenario above. You don't even need a video camera! Some programs, such as iMovie, will allow users to drop in pictures from stills cameras or the Internet, MP3s and other audio files, short video clips, PDF files and a range of other formats. Simple title and text animations combined with easily recorded voice-overs can produce some highly effective multi-media files. For example, in an English literature class, students have to produce a multi-media project which aims to capture the themes and imagery of a selected poem. By com-bining music and images with selected text and maybe even a recital, the students can be challenged to justify (verbally or in writing) their decisions and choices. By engaging with the material in this way, you are providing a new way of experi-encing and analysing poetry.

In our exploration of these emergent technologies there is one essential piece missing, however, and it is fast being recognized as the most influential development of the new digital classrooms and workshops: the interactive whiteboard.

Really smart whiteboards

There are a number of electronic whiteboard options available with names such as ACTIVboard, ELECTROboard, eBoard and SMARTboard. Essentially, they comprise the same three elements (although there are significant differences in their technologies), these are: a projector, an interactive board (like a giant writing tablet) and a computer. These boards are starting to appear everywhere in education, including (it is worth noting) in primary schools. For many of our youngsters today, these exciting new developments are simply part of the everyday furniture of their education, just like tables and chairs. It is a 'normal', even an 'ordinary' experience of learning. In a few years, these children will be teenagers, ready for FE and they will have significantly different expectations when they enrol at college than today's students.

This is not the place to explain in detail how these interactive whiteboards work, or to discuss the merits of each solution (since by the time you have finished reading this page, there will have been several new updates, and at least one more feature added). It is more important to discuss the impact of these devices upon teaching and learning, and consider how the relationships between student, tutor and learning material will undoubtedly undergo a radical transformation within the coming generation.

Many of the interactive whiteboards generally have the following features:

- You can display any file or window from a computer, including Internet pages, slide shows, moving and still images.
- You can drag and drop objects around the screen, navigate the Internet, highlight sections and scroll through pages using your fingers like a mouse.
- You can write on the board using special pens. Some options also include handwriting recognition to turn your scrawl into typeface.
- You can use screen captures and record your interactions for future use.
- You can print your writing or images straight from the board to create instant handouts.
- You can use customized subject specific templates for a range of activities.

There are other features which are unique to each option and, as has already been stated, new features and possibilities and templates are being introduced regularly.

Before we get ahead of ourselves, however, there are two obstacles to overcome with the use of electronic whiteboards in FE, if the transformation agenda is to take hold. The first obstacle is the automatic assumption that these whiteboards are best located in rooms which are already full of PCs, being used simply as an enhancement of IT. The DfES strategy behind the 'Key Skills 2000' (and the updated 'Key Skills 2004') policy has led to a bottleneck of IT resources. Around the country, practically every IT room is timetabled to teach the same hour of word processing, spreadsheets and databases, again and again and again. At the front of the room, you will find a beleaguered IT tutor using the interactive whiteboard to display the same sample spreadsheet, hour after hour after hour. No interactivity, in fact no real activity at all! Interactive whiteboards are seen as part of the IT resource, rather than as a general teaching and learning tool. If you happen to work in a college in which network managers can disproportionately influence strategic infrastructure decisions, then this is almost inevitable. In those colleges where teaching staff have a major say in the IT infrastructure, you are more likely to find these interactive whiteboards in classrooms rather than IT suites. It is not our intention to paint technicians as 'baddies', or suggest a 'them and us' culture exists in every case, but there will naturally be some tension between service providers and service users in a rapidly changing and economically challenged environment.

The second obstacle to overcome is the overuse of Power-Point, as discussed earlier. It is disheartening to see a teacher stand in front of one of these devices and deliver a lecture, especially when they insist on using a mouse to advance the slides. By simply converting your old acetates into animated text you are undermining the creative potential of the resource at your disposal.

The augmented learning environment

As we have seen, there are many exciting new possibilities when a lecturer introduces digital technology into the classroom, and we have discussed just a few examples. This is only really the beginning. The real revolution will happen when the various strands of ILT, ICT and e-learning start to converge.

If you are regularly using a VLE with a group of students and are fortunate enough to be based in a classroom with an interactive whiteboard and have access to wireless laptops (as well as video cameras, stills cameras, microphones and other paraphernalia), then you will be close to creating what we could safely call an 'augmented learning environment' (an ALE). This is an environment that combines the rapid researching and organization of information (through access to online resources) with the creative ability to manipulate, interpret and redesign this material into new forms (using digital resources), as well as the power to share, collect and distribute the results of the investigation (through the interactive whiteboard).

Early experiments with an ALE point the way to real transformation of teaching and learning. For example, in an art history class, the tutor downloads sample images of the pre-Raphaelites onto the whiteboard. A discussion follows and, passing round the tablet PC (linked to the whiteboard), students are encouraged to circle, or identify, common characteristics of the poses, gestures and facial expressions of the subjects. The resulting annotated images are saved though screen captures and uploaded back into the VLE. During the next session, the students refer to these images and take a digital stills camera to compose their own variations of these pre-Raphaelite subjects. These are uploaded, displayed and discussed, with students making comparisons between their own images and images in further samples.

In an aural class, the music tutor uses an MP3 recorder to conduct an experiment. She instructs the class to start clapping in unison. It takes less than 3 seconds for the whole class to fall into a shared rhythm. The recording is played back and the wave form is displayed onto the whiteboard. Discussion follows over how many claps it takes for the rhythm to be established, before the tutor then surprises the class by displaying another waveform from another group that followed the same instruction. They are almost identical! More waveforms are displayed and more examples played. Close analysis shows that in some cases there is only a few milliseconds of difference. The students then use wireless laptops to work though an online learning object and complete an online test at the end of the session. Before they leave the room, the tutor chats to each one briefly about their test results that automatically feed into their individual markbook.

This is not a scene from the future. All of these situations are possible now. The convergence of these various strands of ILT, ICT and e-learning is not commonplace yet, but it is happening increasingly in FE. These developments are ultimately being driven, not by well-meaning managers, and certainly not by the Key Skills IT curriculum, but by the dedication and perseverance of individual teachers who apply creative technology to their subjects, often in very difficult circumstances. However, we are not alone when we move onto the e-learning path, there are a wide range of institutions and resources that we can make use of to help us along the way.

5 Learning resources for FE

Learning resources

Now that you have heard what is possible for e-learning, let's suppose you've decided to introduce e-learning into your lessons. You will need to know what learning resources exist. Where do you begin to find good-quality resources that you can use? Hopefully this section will address some of these issues.

What are learning resources?

The resources that are used for e-learning today can take many forms and can be used across lots of different media. For example, a learning resource could be an e-book or an online database that is used for research. It could be a PowerPoint presentation, a flash animation, a video or an audio file. It could be as simple as an interactive Word document or as sophisticated as a whole course designed to run in a virtual-learning environment. There are so many examples!

What these things have in common is the fact that they are complete objects that can be used to deliver learning on a particular topic. However, many of these learning resources can also be broken down, or disaggregated, into even smaller components, or learning objects, each of which can be repackaged into new learning resources as required. (There is also software available to specifically do this. See Chapter 3 for more details.)

Learning resources are not just confined to the classroom either. Resources for e-learning are used in drop-in IT centres and professional development centres too. The increasing number of students undertaking Distance Education, Open

Learning, and Work-Based Learning need to access the colleges learning resources too.

For cases of remote access like this, students would first have to undergo an authentication process which checks that it is really the student who has permission to access the resources that are about to be used. One example of this is athens, which we will talk more about later. But, for now, it's worth noting that learning resources that are held electronically for e-learning now have a far wider reach than a tutor's handout. When held centrally, it is the availability of these new kinds of resources that allows us to start believing that 'anytime anywhere' learning can occur.

What learning resources currently exist for use within FE?

There are many excellent sources of e-learning resources available for use within FE. These can come from any of a number of providers and they may also be free of charge. As mentioned earlier, resources can take many shapes and forms and so their size, complexity and cost will vary accordingly.

Given that the scope is so wide, the choices on offer regarding the selection of resources to use can sometimes seem a little daunting, but such diversity does mean that there is likely to be something available that generally fits your needs. It simply means that your selection process has to involve looking to the right provider for resources that match your budget, subject level and curriculum area.

Let's begin by looking at some of the key providers and what they offer.

Many resources that are targeted specifically to the FE sector are provided by JISC (Joint Information Systems Committee) (see Chapter 9 on key organizations and sources of help), although they are not the only providers: there are many more. As a key provider, however, JISC does make a good starting point, so let's look at what they have to offer first.

JISC Collections

JISC negotiates for and licenses online materials providing a range of resources to support FE. These agreements bring e-learning resources to the sector at better prices than some commercial providers and with more favourable terms and conditions. This makes JISC Collections an attractive option to colleges who often need to keep learning resource expenditure within tight budgets.

The JISC Collections are a portfolio of electronic resources which are intended to enrich teaching, learning and research. Their collection of resources includes some that are available free of charge and others that JISC subsidizes to provide special low rates for FE institutions.

They provide a diverse range of learning materials including databases, animations, video clips, images, maps and many other useful items. They also support many curriculum areas including fashion, business, media, hairdressing.

Use of the JISC Collections is generally priced according to the number of students in the college. This is done according to JISC bandings which relate to the size of the institution. JISC offer trial periods too, whereby use of the resources will be free for evaluation for anything from one week to one month. Therefore, if there is a new JISC resource that you would like to try, it is often worth asking your learning resource staff if either you or they can evaluate it first free of charge.

Most JISC Collections licences are site licences that allow concurrent access by users across the institution. This offers the best solution, as it means that students across the college should be able to access these e-learning resources at any time.

The resources that are available within your college as part of the JISC Collections will depend on what the college has subscribed to, but listed below are examples of some of the popular subscription ones.

Academic Library (www.theacademiclibrary.com)
This virtual library contains 300 e-book titles covering Anthropology and Development Studies; Cultural and Media Studies; Politics and International Relations, with an additional collection of classic texts in Political Economy.

Britannica Online (www.britannica.co.uk)
Britannica Online is the complete encyclopedia, as well as Merriam-Webster's Collegiate Dictionary and Thesaurus, Britannica Student Encyclopedia and the Britannica Book of the Year.

Creative Club and ADSNAPS (www.creativeclub.co.uk)
Creative Club is the UK's largest advertising archive and it includes over 1,500,000 advertisements across all media. Users are able to search by company, brand or sector, for TV, press, direct mail, outdoor, Internet, cinema and radio ads. ADSNAPS is a quick and easy way to generate product or company reports available in PowerPoint or PDF formats.

Digimap (www.edina.ac.uk/digimap)
Digimap is an EDINA service that delivers Ordnance Survey Map data to UK tertiary education. Data is available either to download to use with appropriate application software such as Graphical Information Systems (GIS) or Computer Aided Design (CAD), or as maps generated by Digimap online.

Early English Books Online (www.eebo.chadwyck.com/home)
Early English Books Online (EEBO) makes available more than 125,000 titles published between 1473 and 1700, starting with the earliest printed works in the English language.

Education Image Gallery (www.edina.ac.uk/eig/index.shtml)
The Education Image Gallery provides access to a collection of 50,000 images covering key events and multiple subject areas including history, entertainment, sport, science, fashion, politics, music, conflict, film, art, leisure and women's studies. You can use the curriculum-related images to illustrate key times, places, people and events.

KnowUK (www.knowuk.co.uk)
KnowUK provides detailed information about the people, institutions and organizations of the United Kingdom.

Other subscription resources
- City Mutual Education has a selection of vocational content at www.cmeducation.co.uk/HTML/index.htm
- GeoProjects resources are vocational too and can be found at www.geoprojects.co.uk
- MINTEL Research reports for Business Studies students can be found at reports.mintel.com
- CHEST don't subsidize like the JISC Collections but they do negotiate good rates for the FE community, available at www.eduserv.org.uk/chest
- Channel 4 and BBC are increasingly offering paid-for resources. See www.channel4.com/learning/ and www.bbc.co.uk/learning

Non-subscription resources
There are also several non-subscription resources that are available for tutors to use. The following are some of the more popular choices.

National Learning Network materials
The National Learning Network (NLN) materials are e-learning resources that are made up of smaller chunks of learning, each taking around 20–30 minutes to complete. They were originally commissioned by BECTA (British Educational Communications and Technology Agency) for the FE sector. These were so well received by practitioners that materials for the Adult and Community Learning sector (ACL) are now also being created.

Currently there are over 500 hours of e-learning material available across a wide range of subjects. The extension to ACL has now also expanded the range to include areas like Family Learning and ESOL.

The materials themselves are not whole courses, but they can be used in lessons as part of a pick-and-mix type approach. They can also be deaggregated and repackaged using a number of content creation tools to make new e-learning resources in their own right. In their current form, the modular make-up of the materials makes them highly suitable for illustrating shorter topics within part of a wider subject area.

The NLN materials were designed to be used within a VLE and in many cases this is how they are employed. However, they are also available on CD-ROM or can be downloaded by specified people within each college, from the NLN materials website directly. You can look at them online yourself but will be asked to register to access. See www.nln.ac.uk/Materials

Resource Discovery Network

The Resource Discovery Network (RDN) is a series of subject-based information gateways or hubs which provide access to more than 100,000 online resources.

The RDN works by compiling resources that have been hand-picked by subject specialists in its partner institutions. These resources are then categorized into subject areas which can be browsed or searched by using key words or phrases. This process of selecting resources by hand ensures that they are of a high quality and that they are appropriate to their particular area. For anyone looking for resources on the Web, it also removes much of the site evaluation that occurs when using an Internet-based search engine. See the following link: www.rdn.ac.uk

RDN Virtual Training Suite

As well as its information gateways, the RDN has also created e-learning resources in the form of a set of tutorials, commonly referred to as the Virtual Training Suite (VTS). The VTS Internet tutorials are available in over 50 subject areas. Like the NLN materials, the suite was originally designed for the FE sector, but it has now been extended to include a set of resources specifically for the ACL sector. See the following link: www.vts.rdn.ac.uk

Access to resources

Now that we know what resources are generally available, it might be useful to outline how these are made available to staff and students within a college.

The most common ways to share learning resources within a college is through a VLE or staff Intranet. This is a structured set of Web pages that is made available internally and used to store important information. These are centralized thereby giving all staff access to the resources that the college has subscribed to or signposted. Of course, the way that a VLE or Intranet is organized will be unique depending on the institution, but generally they will provide links to both subscription and non-subscription resources which the college has signed up to. Invariably, they often house additional resources, in the form of Web links to other useful external sites.

Generally, access to the staff Intranet or VLE will depend on the use of passwords that will have been allocated to staff. In addition, many colleges will also use athens to control access to their resources. athens is an authentication process through which students and staff are issued with passwords which control access to their authorized online resources. Using athens, a student or member of staff can gain access to a resource or service over the Web by entering a username and password.

The athens service is funded by JISC and is free to all colleges. athens is particularly useful when controlling students' remote access to resources and services which the college has subscribed to; such as in the case of a work-based or distance learner.

The effective storage and delivery of learning resources is an important prerequisite for e-learning to occur. Tutors need to have materials to hand that support their classroom delivery and students also need to be able to gain access to many of these remotely. To prevent the duplication of resources, the set-up of the hosting system, whether it is a VLE or an Intranet, will also require a good level of organization. This will differ from one college to the next, but what follows is an example of how the hosting of e-learning resources takes place in one particular college in the West Midlands.

This college currently has 3,000 users accessing a VLE that is set up to cater for over 100 different courses. They use a commercial VLE as a repository for storing e-learning materials, schemes of work, lesson plans and assignment materials. Part of the VLE is set up as a virtual 'common room'. In this area, students can access generic material such as documentation relating to their induction programme, student support materials and resources that support CV writing and basic ICT skills.

Similarly, a separate part of the VLE has been set up as a 'staff room'. This area contains all of the materials that the college currently subscribes to, as well as links to separate external resources.

Finally, a third feature of their VLE arrangement is the presence of separate course areas. Typically, each course has an area that holds resources that are specific to that course. In this area, all tutors associated with this course can upload their own learning resources and allow their own students to access this area to obtain resource relevant to their course.

 Within your college, there may be other ways to find out which resources are available to support your teaching. A few are listed below:

- Articles in monthly or weekly ILT newsletters can be used as a way of highlighting new resources that have been added to the college's collection.
- There may be a dedicated area of the college Intranet or VLE that focuses on learning resources. This can be used to post notices about learning resources as well as offer ideas for using them in the classroom.
- Some staff development training sessions will show tutors how to find and use resources for their curriculum area.
- Messages can be posted on the staff noticeboard or tutors might receive emails informing them of new resources or spotlighting a particular type of resource.
- Tutors may be able to attend external training courses that

show them how they can identify resources on the Web for teaching and learning.

How are learning resources used to support teaching and learning?

Learning resources can be used in any of a number of ways, depending on the creativity of the tutor. Some resources will have been designed to explain a particular topic and for the student to work through independently, whereas other resources will be required to be slotted into another activity. What follows are some examples of each.

The NLN materials are very good at demonstrating particular tasks, making the most of audio, video and flash animation. As such, they can be linked to from a separate document and used to illustrate key points. One example in which this could be used is for a demonstration of how to clean a fish. This e-learning module shows visually how this is done, rather than the student having to scale and gut an actual fish.

A second example of the use of a particular type of e-learning resource might be encouraging your students to use Newsbank or Infotrak to look at current news topics. They could be set the task of referring to the UK edition of *The Times*, and then to a copy of the *New York Times* to observe the international angles of each newspaper. This could be a useful exercise for media studies students. See, for example, www.newsbank. com/UK/nbnp_uk.html and www.galeuk.com/jisc/index.htm

Using the above examples, a tutor may have the opportunity to bring library staff into lessons to support students' searching activities or use of individual learning resources. For example, using Infotrak or Newsbank they could help the student to develop their information literacy and information retrieval skills, both of which are important skills to have in today's society. Working closely with the library staff should be encouraged, and perhaps crafting a separate lesson to demonstrate some of the available learning resources is worth doing in its own right. These information literacy and information retrieval skills will prove essential if a student progresses on to higher education, where it will be important to be able to interrogate a database and to use a library catalogue. They are also useful general skills to acquire.

Sometimes activities can be based around the structure of the learning resources. For example, consider a database that catalogues learning resources. Information technology students who are studying database design may also benefit from an examination of the structure of the database as well as interrogating its content for their studies. In this case, the database itself, rather than its contents, becomes the actual learning resource.

There are many other examples of ways in which learning resources are used in the classroom and no two tutors will necessarily use each resource in the same way. It is down to the individual to decide which item best suits the task they have to hand or best conveys the information they wish to get across to their students.

New case studies are being produced all the time to show ways that learning resources are used to support teaching and learning, and lots of these are accessible on the Web. A good starting point is the Ferl website for examples of how practitioners are using general resources. This is a good first choice because here you can also download and access new learning resources that practitioners have created themselves and sub-mitted to the Ferl resource library. See the following links: ferl.becta.org.uk/ and ferl.becta.org.uk/display.cfm?catID=1

The NLN materials site will have more information about the ways in which the NLN materials are being used within colleges. And, at the time of writing, JISC are in the process of putting together lists of exemplars, i.e. case studies which highlight how materials taken from their collections are being used.

There are currently five exemplars covering the following subjects:

1. History
2. Leisure
3. Hairdressing
4. Business
5. Skills for Life.

If you are based within an education institution you can access these exemplars online at http://restricted.jisc.ac.uk/ exemplars_fe/

Hopefully, this chapter has introduced you to a number of resources which might prove useful in your teaching and learning. But don't forget that this list is constantly changing as new resources are released by external providers, or your college subscribes to new content. You can keep up to date by asking your learning resource staff for recommendations based on your curriculum area. The pool of resources that is available will also change as colleagues within your college increasingly create and share their resources too. Finally, if there is nothing or very little available that matches your specific requirements, rather than be put off from the idea of using e-learning materials, I hope you will refer to Chapter 3 and have a go at designing some materials of your own!

6 Keeping tidy: VLEs *et al.*

You, me and our VLE

We referred to VLEs in general terms in the previous chapter but what can they really do for us? VLE stands for Virtual Learning Environment, no doubt a hang-up from the 1990s when practically everything to do with computers had 'virtual' or 'cyber' as a prefix, and indeed this is when the first VLEs were being introduced into progressive American universities. If they had been introduced more recently, after the millennium, they would no doubt be prefixed with a small 'e' or (if you want to be really cool and streetwise) a small 'i'. Things have progressed significantly since those first clumsy attempts at putting course materials online, but the name stuck, and although there are attempts now to replace the VLE with the MLE (Managed Learning Environment) which ties up the educational functionality of the VLE with data handling functions of MIS, it seems that VLE is entering the dictionary of FE speak. Some bright spark has even started speaking about 'ALEs' (Augmented Learning Environments) which integrates the VLE, MIS, digital classroom, streaming video and wireless technology into a single convergent solution. Enough . . .

Every computer is 'my' computer

What is a VLE? In Chapter 5 we showed how one college was using a VLE with 3,000 students to act as a repository for information relevant to specific courses, but how did they achieve this in practice? Quite simply, a VLE is a way of sharing teaching and learning resources, setting assignments and providing feedback, organizing materials and data in such a way that students can access these online through the Internet.

Imagine that any handout you have ever passed round, any PowerPoint presentation you have ever made or any assignment you ever set (complete with grades of every student you ever assessed) could be instantly available to you anywhere in the world (with an Internet connection) at any time. No need for floppies, hard copies, USB (Universal Serial Bus) memory sticks or CD-RWs (CD-Rewriters). Even better, no need for filing cabinets, lever-arch files, staplers and photocopiers (yes I did say 'no need for photocopiers'!). Imagine that within minutes you could be in a computer environment that is totally familiar to you, with everything where you left it. You walk into a classroom and 'boom', up comes the PowerPoint of today's topic. You arrive home and sit down at your computer and 'boom', progress reviews and markbooks are there in a flash. You pop into the library and 'boom', someone has left you a 'thanks for being a funky teacher' message on the noticeboard. Suddenly, it doesn't matter which computer you use, they all look and feel the same. No more, 'It's on my computer at home' or 'My floppy doesn't open'. Your bit of cyberspace goes with you to any access point. Every computer is your computer, and it is backed-up for you every day.

If used to its full capabilities, a VLE can be a transforming experience for a teacher. I used to watch a drama tutor, Richard, struggle every day with two briefcases and at least three carrier bags full of files and paper. Every morning, he would arrive in the car park and make his journey (sometimes two journeys) to the staffroom laden with paperwork and marking. At the end of the day he would take it all home again. With shoulders bent, downcast eyes and lolloping gait; like Marley's Ghost dragging the chains of FE through the night air. Recently, I saw him walking into work with a spring in his step, hands swinging freely and listening to early English madrigals on an MP3 player. 'What happened?' I asked. He ignored me. He couldn't hear me because of the MP3 player, but later I found out that he had spent the last year grappling with the VLE and it was beginning to pay off.

Doing the same job twice

As Richard would testify, when starting out with a VLE, it is difficult to trust its capabilities. For example, you will write an online assignment and create a back-up in Word, which you will then printout, photocopy and file somewhere. This is perfectly understandable and predictable. We have become so bound up with the world of paper that we somehow think that paperwork is an essential element of teaching and learning. (If you responded with 'Well it is' then we are all doomed!) My friend Richard is a living testimony to this. It was six months after having committed to the VLE that he stopped producing hard copies for his files (which he never looked at anyway). 'I was doing each job twice: once the old way, and once the new way. The VLE was making life harder. Once I stopped doing it the old way, it was like a great weight being lifted.' I pointed out to Richard that this was because he didn't have to carry all his files backwards and forwards from home. He didn't even raise an eyebrow: 'Now that I trust the VLE and am familiar with it, I find that I work much faster and spend very little time looking for things. It's really easy . . .'

A VLE wishlist

As a way of discussing the features of a VLE, I have sought to provide a list of things to look for, as if you were planning to buy one. The following is a wish list of features that appear in various combinations from the various providers.

Customizabilty

This word is yet to find its way into most dictionaries, but in the tradition of current IT speak, we take Shakespeare's approach of popularizing new words or making up our own if there isn't one to suit our needs. Many VLEs allow users to select which features to include. There are a selection of tools from which to choose, depending on how you plan to use the VLE. These could be drawn from the options below, or could include others not listed here. For example, you might wish to include a calendar and a library of resources, but not want to include a markbook. You can build your toolset in much the same way you select which toolbars to see in Word.

Interoperability

Another big word favoured by the geeks. If you are using a VLE, meeting interoperability standards means that it needs to be able to communicate with other systems, and work equally well with the growing variety of browsers and platforms.

Uploading

It should be possible with any VLE to place documents and other files into online folders that can be accessed by other staff and students or just by yourself. You should be able to control access rights to these folders so they can only be scrutinized by people you choose. Uploading these should simply be a matter of a few clicks. Being able to rename, copy and organize these folders in a meaningful way is a common feature of all good VLEs.

WebDAV is a recent development of operating systems that allows for the creation of Web folders. This feature allows for much easier uploading and management of online resources. You have a folder on your computer that looks and works like any other folder except that it links directly to an online server. Rather than having to upload materials through your Web browser, you can open this folder on your computer, drag files to it, move them around and delete them as you like, making instant adjustments to the online materials. The potential for this development is only now beginning to be realized by many of the VLE providers and will dramatically speed up the process of sharing resources and making them available.

Assignments

There are essentially three types of assignments: offline work, online work and electronic tests.

Offline assignments

Offline assignments are what we do all the time. Whenever a student hands something in to you, makes something, demonstrates a skill, sits a written exam or makes a presentation, then they are working 'offline'.

Online assignments

An online assignment is one which is submitted electronically (e.g. via email or other system). This is likely to be a word-processed document but in theory could be any electronic file (MP3, video clip, flash movie, jpeg, etc.). When freed from the limitations of the world of paper, and providing that the curriculum allows such flexibility, the concept of the 'assignment' can also be liberated. For example, isn't a video journal shot on a student's mobile phone and submitted as coursework as valid as a written diary, if it addresses the appropriate issues and makes the same points? For many NVQs and diplomas, the video evidence has always been possible, but the technology has previously been highly specialized and expensive, and consequently difficult to support. Now dozens of these devices can be found in every classroom, and your students will leap at the chance to use them.

Electronic tests

The third type of assignment is the online assessment in which students will, for example, take tests that are automatically marked and scored. If you use multiple-choice assessments at all in your teaching, then this feature alone is worth the effort. Imagine: you create the assessment once and it can be used time and time again. And you never have to mark it! You, and your students, get accurate and instant feedback on the results. This is an example of computers finally doing the things they have always promised.

Markbooks

You can store the results from tests and assignments and provide written feedback online to your students. Typically, a student can only see their own markbook, but staff can see all the students' markbooks. The markbook system automatically records when the work was handed in, when it was marked, when the feedback was written, when it was resubmitted and remarked and so on. It can collate this information and provide you with instantly updated student progress. If you want to know how well a student is doing, look at the markbook. If a student is falling behind, the evidence is there. This way you can spot the 'at risk' student quickly and address the problem.

Diaries and calendars

If you set an assignment or arrange a field trip, then the dates for these should automatically feed into the student's login window or homepage. You should be able to use these calendars at an individual level, a course level and even an institutional level. A well-managed calendar can become a great asset to course delivery and the main advantage of VLE-based calendars over traditional paper-based calendars is the ability to make changes which are instantaneous and fed automatically to the recipients.

Email accounts

Suddenly having one email account is not enough. Such has been the explosion of the email culture that the minimum number of accounts an FE tutor needs is four. One for friends and family, one for work (staff), one for exchanges with students and one for membership of all those Internet sites that send out passwords, invoices and account details. The earlier we start to keep these various strands of our lives separate, the more likely we are to retain our sanity. If the VLE solution you work with includes an email option, then the third strand is taken care of.

Discussion groups and forums

A popular feature of many Web communities is the ability to host discussion groups or forums in which members of an interest group can share views and have questions answered. In reality, although membership is large for many of these forums, there is a tendency for them to be dominated by a core membership who make regular postings, with the rest of us only contributing occasionally. A properly managed discussion group within a VLE can be a novel way of covering outcomes and generating evidence for selected topics.

Chat rooms and instant messaging

Many colleges prohibit the use of instant messaging and chat room services, but many VLE solutions have this as an optional extra. There is limited educational value within the classroom, but it allows for elements of a programme or course to be delivered through distance learning and could open new possibilities for local community, national and even international tutorial support.

Video conferences

The technology for video conferencing over the Internet and through 3G (Third Generation) mobile phones is still very much in its infancy, although broadband and new compression technology will enable much higher-quality video interaction in the not too distant future. Combined with online presentations and interactive whiteboards, it is possible to deliver lectures and hold seminars with little technical knowledge and no special software other than your usual browser.

Resources and links

Do you remember when libraries would put together resource packs on a selected topic by gathering newspaper articles, book lists, images and other materials and placing them into a single folder? Some of you may even still be doing it! ILT literacy enables this activity to be done online by gathering links to selected websites and subject gateways, image galleries, presentations and a host of interactive materials. These can also be organized into topic folders to be accessed by staff and students as part of larger projects. For example, each of the themes for 'Every Child Matters' could be addressed through online tutorial packs of learning materials and online resources that can be accessed by personal tutors as a part of a planned cross-college programme.

Learning content creation

A growing number of free tools are available for ILT confident tutors that enable you to create your own interactive materials. These include quizzes, word searches, Web-page creation, picture matching and crosswords, some of which are described in Chapter 3. Some VLEs are building these tools into their functionality so that they can be developed within a familiar environment in a managed way. An example here would be a simple revision exercise covering key concepts and vocabularies for a selected topic. The tutor creates some very straightforward Web pages including text and images followed by a crossword and picture matching exercise to reinforce learning. These materials are all created through a managed process (like a wizard) which creates the materials to a set format and style.

Shared documents

In group work, it is possible with some providers to create contributory documents that each group member can share and add to, thereby building their own resource base for projects. They can be opened, edited and added to by any member of any group that you choose to specify.

Tutorials, targets and individual learning plans (ILPs)

Some VLE solutions have started to introduce the ability to set and monitor targets and produce learning plans that are stored online and can be seen by the student and modified by staff. No need to send home reports when both students and parents can have access to a constantly updating progress review which details when the targets were set, when they are due for review and when they have been completed.

Release dates

If you have gathered all your resources for the year and uploaded them all onto the VLE, you may not want your students to be able to have access to these resources all at once. Some options allow you to plan windows of availability in advance so that these resources are released to students at staged intervals, thereby allowing control of materials similar to the way in which you would release traditional handout materials. No teacher would walk into class, give out everything on the first day and expect students to be able to cope with all the information at once.

Security

Obviously, with all this information being stored online, you may well be dealing with some very sensitive or confidential data. You should be able to set access rights to folders and data so that it is only viewable by those who have been given access. The range of possibilities varies considerably from having no access, through being able to see but not alter, add but not delete, to total control of content. Passwords become increasingly important, but it isn't just your password that needs protecting: anyone who has the same access rights also needs to be aware of the need for security, and in large organizations the possibilities for hackers to gain access to sensitive data becomes relatively easy if some staff don't bother to change from the default password!

A convergent future

All of the above features are available now on at least one VLE, and there are more features that haven't been listed. But it is also true that as yet no single VLE offers all of the features identified.

There are more VLEs out there than you can imagine and it is not the purpose of this book to promote one solution over another. It is also unlikely that you will be directly involved in deciding which VLE your institution invests in. Besides, each of the commercial companies (and even some so-called 'open-source' solutions) have strong sales teams who will gladly offer you free trials if you show even the slightest interest. It is also true that such is the competition in the VLE market that even before you have finished reading this chapter, you can be assured that at least one of the companies will have introduced an update that adds some new functionality to their VLE (or at least solves one of its many problems).

As the competition continues, it is likely that many of the VLE providers will 'borrow' successful features from other providers and discard other, less successful or user-unfriendly elements. In time, the provision of a 'standard' may well emerge, based on customizable toolsets that offer easy-to-use popular features. The process of convergence will mean ultimately that the choice over which VLE to adopt will be based more on how the features are integrated than on what features they possess.

If you are interested in exploring the various VLE options and your institution has yet to decide which one to go for, then you might want to explore some of the options below and share your thoughts with the decision-makers.

VLE options

Blackboard @ www.blackboard.com/uki/
A well-known and popular American suite of applications and products favoured by some HE institutions in the UK. Recently merged with WebCT.

CourseManager @ www.coursemanager.com
Another US solution that offers products geared to online and distance learning.

DigitalBrain @ corporate.digitalbrain.com/index.php
Chosen by the London Grid for Learning (LGfL), this UK based VLE provider also has a presence in many schools and colleges.

Fronter @ fronter.co.uk/uk
Scandanavian in origin but with a strong UK presence, this VLE emphasizes scalability and collaborative tools.

Learnwise @ www.learnwise.com
Part of the Granada (ITV plc) group, this is proving to be a popular choice for FE colleges in the UK, as well as some HE institutions.

Moodle @ moodle.org
This is probably one of the best-known free open-source solutions available for course management and online learning. It is modular in its structure so you can build it piece by piece.

VirtualCampus (www.teknical.com/products/ virtualcampusv5.htm)
A propriety VLE solution favoured by the aviation industry. It is easy to get a guest log-in so you can explore the features for yourself.

WebCT (www.webct.com/entrypage)
Previously a competitor of Blackboard in the US, now merged, but still with a distinct identity, but who knows for how long?

Other alternatives
When you have tried those and feel hungry for more:

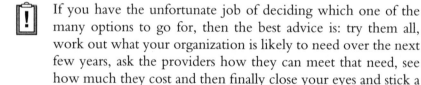

Angel Learning	www.angellearning.com
Desire2Learn	www.desire2learn.com
eCollege	www.ecollege.com
Jenzabar	www.jenzabar.com
Plateau	www.plateau.com

If you have the unfortunate job of deciding which one of the many options to go for, then the best advice is: try them all, work out what your organization is likely to need over the next few years, ask the providers how they can meet that need, see how much they cost and then finally close your eyes and stick a pin in the list!

7 Levelling the field: accessibility in ICT

Accessibility is an important issue for e-learning, as it recognizes that some students have certain visual, auditory or other physical impairments which prevent them from being able to access materials or resources. It draws attention to these issues and focuses us on what we need to do, individually and on an institutional level, to try to make sure individual needs are catered for.

Disability legislation

Accessibility is so important that it is now addressed within current legislation under the wider umbrella of disability. The rights and responsibilities of colleges are guided by two significant acts, the *Special Educational Needs and Disabilities Act 2001* (SENDA) and the *Disability Discrimination Act 1995 (DDA)*.

The *Disability Discrimination Act* makes it unlawful for colleges to discriminate against disabled students and other disabled people. Colleges have been subject to this Act (as employers and as providers of goods and services) since 1996 but in 2001 their legal obligations were extended with the introduction of SENDA. The *Special Educational Needs and Disabilities Act 2001* became Part 4 of the DDA, stating that:

- colleges and Local Education Authorities (LEAs) must not treat disabled students less favourably for a reason relating to their disability;
- colleges and LEAs must ensure they provide reasonable adjustments for disabled learners.

In terms of e-learning, this roughly translates to the need for a constant examination of areas that affect students' access to learning, including learning resources, online learning provision and the college's wider use of ILT. The college now has a legal obligation to ensure that these areas are as accessible as possible. Where additional services or products are bought in, the same responsibility extends to the consideration of these.

The requirements of Part 4 of the DDA are also referred to as 'anticipatory', meaning that staff have a responsibility to consider the needs of disabled students *before* they arise: it's simply not enough to make adjustments after the fact. In reality, however, this can be an arduous task since it asks us to predict what needs might arise. How would a tutor know, for example, that one of their students might have difficulty reading red text on the screen? Well let's face it, unless they were told, they might not, but the legislation states that they should merely try to anticipate it (in this case, perhaps, in the selection of appropriate learning resources). The key lies in striving to be as inclusive as possible and considering all eventualities in everyday activity.

Who does the DDA relate to?
The DDA states that a disabled student is someone who has a physical or mental impairment which has an effect on his/her ability to carry out normal day-to-day activities. The effect must be substantial, adverse and long term, i.e. lasting more than 12 months. Its definition includes people with sensory or physical impairments, dyslexia, medical conditions, mental-health difficulties and learning difficulties. We will discuss specific cases of these and how they might be catered for later.

Of course, it's not always possible to know that students fall into any of these categories but it is important that all colleges take appropriate steps to encourage students to disclose this type of information. This is usually done during the enrolment process.

Who has the responsibility for accessibility?
In summary, everyone who supports students does. Of course, the many roles within a college are very diverse, but everyone has a part to play in ensuring that they do what they can, within

their area of expertise, to ensure that students' needs are appropriately catered for.

This often involves a significant investment in staff training on the part of the college, to ensure that appropriate methods of achieving inclusive responses to student needs are disseminated to all staff. Any training programme should cover the key issues within current legislation, and should outline ways in which these issues will be addressed through the everyday policies and procedures of the institution. The training should provide a generic overview of accessibility and introduce all staff to what this means. But there will still be additional things that specific staff members can do, depending on their job roles. In the area of e-learning, tutors should have the choice of both hardware and software solutions to assist in their teaching and ensure that students' needs are met. The choices of solutions will depend exclusively on what the college has invested in but we will discuss some of the more popular solutions below.

Low-tech vs high-tech solutions

All colleges will have a range of IT accessibility solutions at their disposal, with some being more complex than others. With regards to accessibility, these solutions will be loosely labelled as 'high-tech' or 'low-tech', depending on their level of complexity.

You will find that some of the most commonly employed accessibility techniques within colleges are those that are the simplest to implement and cost the least (in fact most cost nothing at all). These are referred to as low-tech solutions. Their relative popularity is down to the fact that they are techniques or quick fixes that can usually be implemented with the minimum amount of fuss and do not require the installation or purchasing of additional software or hardware.

On the other hand, high-tech solutions, found at the other end of the spectrum, will often require the purchase and installation of special types of software and significantly more investment in terms of time and money. In some cases, high-tech solutions will also require third-party support, either externally or from the college's own IT department.

Whether high-tech or low-tech, the additional support made

available to students could be a software solution, a hardware solution or a combination of both. Listed below are some of the ways that software can be used to support the students' use of ILT.

Software solutions

There are a number of ways that the software already available on the students' PCs can be used to make learning material more accessible to them and the PCs customized according to their personal preferences. These quick and easy fixes are ideal, as they allow students to change or customize features based on their unique needs. This is an important aspect of accessibility – it's not just about making large adjustments for a small number of users, it's about making small changes for a larger number of users too, so that everyone's ILT experiences can be maximized.

To begin, let's look at customizing a student's browser to suit their preferences.

Customizing Internet Explorer

There are some relatively simple changes that can be made within Internet Explorer (version 5 and above) to help some students access material on the Web. The following are some of the kinds of things that can be changed within Internet Options from the Tools menu.

- Font size – a student can use this option to change the font size displayed in the browser. (Note you can also change the text size of the font displayed on a website on your browser's 'view' menu.)
- Font settings – this can be used to select a different font type.
- Colour settings – using this feature, a student can change the colours of the page background, text and links to suit their preferences.

TechDis User Preferences Toolbar

TechDis have also recently released their User Preferences Toolbar which provides tutors and students with a simple way of imposing accessibility preferences onto potentially any Web page. You can access the toolbar at www.techdis.ac.uk/index.php?p=1_20051905100544

Windows accessibility options

Windows has a special menu offering accessibility options (found in Start > Programs > Accessories). There it offers a selection of programs that will enhance accessibility using software built into the Windows environment. Below are some of the most commonly used ones:

Magnifier

Magnifier enlarges a portion of the screen for easier viewing. It creates a separate window that displays a magnified portion of the screen. The student can then choose to change the colour scheme of the magnification window for easier visibility or he/she can move or resize the Magnifier window, to suit their particular preferences.

Narrator

Narrator uses text-to-speech technology to read the contents of the screen aloud. Unfortunately, the voices used are not very natural, but it can still be a useful feature for students who are blind or visually impaired.

On-Screen Keyboard

The On-Screen Keyboard is a utility that displays a virtual keyboard on the screen and allows users with mobility impairments to type data using a pointing device or joystick.

Accessibility options in control panel

There are accessibility options available from within the Windows control panel which are useful for customizing the way that a student's keyboard, display or mouse functions.

Sticky keys
This feature can be useful if a student has trouble holding down one or more keys simultaneously. For example, where a shortcut needs you to hold down two keys, with this feature turned on, you could click the first key and then its modifier (usually CTRL, SHIFT, ALT or Windows key (the one with the small flap on it, normally next to the Alt Key)) without having to press both at the same time.

Filter keys
When this option is selected, Windows will ignore brief or repeated key strokes or slow the repeat rate. This is a useful feature for students who have manual dexterity problems.

Toggle keys
When the toggle key option is activated, a student will hear sounds when any of the locking keys are pressed (caps lock, scroll lock or number lock). A high beep will indicate that the key has been turned on, and a low one will signal it being turned off. This can prove useful for anyone with a visual impairment or certain kinds of cognitive disabilities.

Mouse keys
This is another accessibility feature that would be useful for students who have difficulty using a mouse. This built-in feature uses the numeric keypad to control the movement of the mouse pointer.

High contrast
This feature is designed for people who have various types of visual impairment. It is another accessibility feature that is available from within the accessibility options found in the control panel. High contrast works by increasing legibility for students by heightening screen contrast with alternative colour combinations. Some of the schemes also change font sizes for greater legibility. All the above accessibility options can be activated through the Accessibility Options in Control Panel.

More complex software solutions

What we have discussed so far are the low-tech solutions which can be implemented by the student him/herself immediately with no charge. We will now go on to examine some of the types of software which offer a higher degree of complexity. These will invariably be software packages that the college has to purchase externally.

Screen Readers

A Screen Reader is a piece of software that will be used by students with visual disabilities. It uses hardware and software to create synthesized voice output for whatever text is displayed on the screen or whatever keys are pressed on the keyboard. Jaws is an example of a popular screen reader, although there are other choices available.

Word-prediction software

Word-prediction technology will predict the words that a student is typing based on word frequency and context. This is a common feature of many mobile phones. Word-prediction software used on a PC may also spellcheck as a student types and, depending on its complexity, also include some speech synthesis.

Speech-recognition software

Speech-recognition software allows a student to generate text by talking into a microphone instead of typing it on the keyboard. By wearing a headset with a microphone in the front, he/she is able to dictate text as well as use editing and formatting commands. The current drawback with a lot of voice-recognition software is that many have to be trained to recognize dialect and accents. However, with patience, they can be trained to recognize the user's voice. Two popular choices of speech-recognition software are Dragon Naturally Speaking and IBM's Via Voice.

Hardware solutions

There are several hardware solutions available which offer the student an alternative method of input.

Trackballs

A trackball is a pointing device that looks slightly like an upside-down mouse, but with the ball sticking out more. To use it, the student rolls the ball with their thumb, fingers, or the palm of their hand. This moves the cursor on the screen in the same way as a mouse. Trackballs come in a range of sizes, from a large device with a ball the size of a ping-pong ball to a handheld device with a small thumb-operated rollerball.

Alternative keyboards

The choice of alternative keyboards should be made available for students with physical disabilities who cannot use a standard keyboard. The range might include smaller keyboards (for students with a reduced range of motion), larger keyboards (for students without fine motor control) or one-handed keyboards which are useful for those who can only type with one hand.

Designing accessible Web-based resources

We have discussed ways that students can access resources using alternative methods but it is equally important to ensure that those resources are accessible.

So what can you do to make sure your resources are more accessible? By adopting just a few basic principles in the design of your resources, you could find you are making a difference to a lot of people. The suggestions here focus on Web-based resources but many are design principles which could also apply to the design of Word documents, particularly if they are intended to be accessed online.

- Use headings to break a Web page or document into suitable sections. Some students using screen readers will navigate through the document using its headings and subheadings as markers.
- Attach an 'alt tag' (a text description) to all graphics. This

is particularly useful to those unable to see the graphic itself or who might be using a screen reader.

- Try to ensure there is a good level of contrast between the text and its background colour. Also try not to use colour to differentiate sections or items on a page as this can cause problems for those with visual impairments.
- Try to avoid having links to items that open in a new window as this can confuse a screen reader. Similarly if a link is to a file in an alternative format, e.g. a PDF (portable document format) file, this should also be indicated in the hyperlink text.
- Spell check your document thoroughly and avoid using abbreviations and acronyms if possible. These will be picked up by a screen reader and can sometimes make no sense at all when pronounced to the user.

There are a number of websites which have been set up to help in the design of accessible Web pages. One of the most common of these is WebXACT. This is a free tool which will check through a Web page and detail any issues it finds in a report. The free version is limited to just checking a single page but it can offer some useful information and highlight some key issues. This will include a list of errors that have been automatically picked up by WebXACT as well as other more general guidelines for the user to check. WebXACT can't be guaranteed to pick up all potential problems, but it can serve as a useful tool. It can be accessed on the Web at www.webxact.watchfire.com

As well as using this tool there are other things you can do yourself to check that your documents are more accessible. For example: can you navigate right through the document with the keyboard? Is the font size adjusted using the options available? Are there any abbreviations used which might need an explanation?

Some of these activities might seem somewhat arduous but it's worth remembering that not only are you designing resources that support disabled users, but also you are adopting principles of good Web design. By making small changes and continuing to implement these principles in your resource design you will be adopting methods of good practice and ensuring that a wider number of people can access your materials.

Additional help

There are many sources of help to advise and guide you through the complex maze of accessibility and inclusion. Some of these will be internal to your college, but many will be outside sources of help which exist primarily to advise on accessibility generally. There are also many websites that support these areas and provide good reference points for staff who want more information on a particular topic. Remember many of these sources of support have been covered in Chapter 5, but below are some specialist ones which offer dedicated support in this area:

TechDis (www.techdis.ac.uk)
TechDis is a JISC-funded educational advisory service working in the field of accessibility and inclusion.

TechDis has recently produced a series of staff packs which can be used for staff development sessions or as a resource for tutors to find out more about accessibility. They are written in a really user-friendly style and can therefore also be used by staff who want to work through the training materials independently.

AbilityNet (www.abilitynet.org.uk)
The AbilityNet website is full of resources and links for accessibility-related materials. The site also has a unique section for Factsheets and Skillsheets which give detailed information on a wide range of assistive technology, services and organizations that can help you get the most out of IT.

AbilityNet has also produced a separate website, My Computer, My Way which will lead you through several options for making your computer easier to use. You can access My Computer, My Way on the Web at www.abilitynet.org.uk/ myway

Help is at Hand

The Help is at Hand website offers a long list of tips about ways for making (Windows) PCs more accessible to students in really simple ways. You can read these on the Web at www.helpisat hand.gov.uk/resources/teaching-learning/groups/disabilities/tips

8 Out and about

Mobile technologies can allow us to extend our armoury of teaching techniques in two major ways; firstly, they let us use ILT outside the normal college environment. Secondly, they enable us to take learning out onto the streets, into the community or even out into the fields. In other words, they can give us the means to deliver e-learning in places where such facilities may not normally be available and to students who may not normally have access to this method of learning.

As the name 'mobile technologies' implies, their greatest advantage is mobility. Currently, FE has concentrated on laptops as its main way of integrating e-learning into locations which don't have access to college networks. Even now, a version of laptop known as a Tablet PC is being seen as the next step in integrating mobile learning into teaching and learning. Some colleges, however, are tapping into the huge potential of even smaller handheld devices which may revolutionize the way we look at e-learning. These devices are already familiar both to us and our students, in some cases too familiar – mobile phones.

So what's available to us at the moment?

The range basically falls into five categories: laptops, tablets, handheld PCs, mobile phones and smartphones, although there is a lot of blurring at the edges between each type of device. You could even include memory sticks and MP3 players into the mix if you wish – many of your students already have! Let's try to understand what each of these gadgets is and what each one can do for us.

Laptops

Most staff within FE should already be familiar with laptops, as they are rapidly becoming the preferred device for many lecturing staff. Their main advantage from the viewpoint of a tutor is that you can carry your electronic workspace around with you. This means that you can finish off that piece of work at home, or while you are on the train, or, if you are really sad, you can do some extra preparation while you are away on holiday!

Another advantage is that you can prepare that PowerPoint presentation on your own machine and (provided you are teaching in a room which has a projector fitted or you can get one to take along with you) you can then go and deliver your presentation straight from your own machine. This even applies in areas where your college network isn't available to you.

However, from an e-learning point of view, laptops have much more potential than that. You can get your students to use laptops – under proper supervision – involving them much more in their own learning. If your college has a teaching set of laptops, it can mean that you have a lot of the functionality of a computer classroom available to you and your students, both inside college and out in the community. In theory, this is a huge step forward, but the practice can be rather different.

Laptops are great when you use them individually, but can be a real problem as a class-teaching tool unless you have the backup services to get them all in place for you. In institutions where there is a well-organized team of technical support staff, a teaching set of laptops can be used very effectively. The tutor books the teaching set over the college's Intranet via an electronic booking system and the technicians have the set all wired up and ready for use as the tutor walks into the room.

The problems occur when the tutor does not have this backup and has to go and collect the teaching set and set them up themselves. Just to move a set of laptops around a campus can be a real pain. Even the lighter ones weigh a significant amount collectively, and then there's all the leads and wires that go with them. You might think that you only need to carry the laptop itself and that it can be charged up for use overnight. However, one of the main problems with using laptops as a

ol is that the battery life can be very limited and
...tery has gone, then, more often than not, you end
.ing to plug in the power pack each time you use laptops
. a teaching session. This process can take a considerable
amount of time and, once the session is finished, you then have
to pack the laptops and the accessories away again.

If you want to use the software already installed on the
machines and to get your students to build a file up from a
blank page it can be relatively easy, but what if you want to use
a file that you have prepared yourself to illustrate some point or
focus some activity? How do you get it onto each of the laptops
quickly, and, once the students have created their work of art,
how do you get it off the laptops so that they can make use of it
elsewhere?

With wireless networking, this can be done fairly quickly,
but what if, as in most colleges, you don't have access to a
wireless network, or you are setting up a teaching set away from
base and away from any sort of network point? I have found
one of the best ways is to use a simple camera card reader – the
sort that allows you to plug in your digital camera flash card and
download your images. These cards now hold up to a gigabyte
of data and you can carry them around in your pocket.

In a recent session, I found that I had forgotten to put the
correct files onto my laptops but fortunately I had a copy on my
flash card. The files included a chunky video and came to
around 40 megabytes. I expected to have to quickly rethink my
session, as the class would be waiting for ages whilst I went
from laptop to laptop copying the information across and
feeling like a lemon! However, using my card reader plugged
into the USB port of the laptops, I managed to copy across all
40 megabytes in just 25 seconds! Since then, I've used it often
as my main data transfer device. Card readers also have
the advantage that if a student manages to foul up one of
your carefully designed exercise files (deliberately or not!), it
takes a matter of seconds to reinstall your unblemished files for
them.

You could also use a memory stick or a pen drive for this
task. These marking pen-sized devices can also hold up to 4
gigabytes of data and most students use them in preference to

floppy disks. After all, why carry around half a dozen disks when you can fit a memory stick into your pocket?

A teaching set of laptops also needs to be stored somewhere. Even 10 laptops plus all the wires, battery packs, etc. that go with them can take up a lot of space, and how do you keep them charged up? One answer is to store them in a specially designed laptop cabinet which often comes on wheels so that it can be trundled from one room to another – OK if you are using them somewhere near to where you keep them stored, but a bit of a problem if they need to go to another campus or if the corridors aren't easy to push a trolley along! And don't forget the time involved in taking all the laptops out and downloading the files that you want to use onto them – that can be quite a task in itself!

Tablets

Tablet PCs or tablets are a variation on the laptop that have the advantage of being slightly less bulky and allowing the student to input information by means of a stylus. This links to a handwriting recognition system that can make inputting notes very similar to writing them out. Unfortunately, unless the student has their own personal tablet, the handwriting recognition can be a bit hit and miss!

Because of the problems outlined above, some e-learning practitioners are becoming increasingly interested in the use of handheld computers or PDAs.

Handheld PCs

Handhelds are small computers that were originally designed to be used as electronic versions of your desk diary. You might also hear them referred to as Personal Digital Assistants (PDAs) or Pocket PCs. They are increasingly being used as an educational e-learning tool that can literally fit in your pocket and yet have much of the capability of their larger desktop cousins. One big plus from the FE viewpoint is their relatively low cost and portability. Instead of that big computer cabinet or a car full of laptops you can still have a lot of computing power with you but carry it into a classroom in a large carrier bag!

PDAs can be used for such diverse activities as taking

ı notes whilst out on a field trip, reviewing video
⌐ correct way to carry out practical tasks, using the
ıacilities to enhance understanding of language, even
⌐ıng PDA-sized Web pages to preview or review lecture
content. This is an area that is still undergoing development and
many more uses will be found as more people use the devices.
This whole area is referred to as 'm-learning' (mobile-learning)
as it enables tutors to use devices away from the classroom or
institution.

One of the main advantages of PDAs over laptops is that as
they are so much cheaper you may feel that you don't need to
be using them for a full session to keep your managers happy.
You can just use them at specific points to enhance your students' understanding of a particular topic.

Most PDAs have a slot that takes a compact flash card – the
same sort that is used in a digital camera. This means that you
could even provide each student with their own card to use as
their electronic workbook for your section of the course.

What can one of these small devices actually do? Well, the
Windows Mobile versions have a cut-down Microsoft Office
built into them which can handle word-processor and spreadsheet files. Database, presentation and acrobat files can also be
fairly easily handled by downloading free software off the Web.
Macromedia flash files can also be used, along with simple Web
pages and sound files such as MP3s. All in all this means that
there is a wide range of potential uses that a tutor can put these
devices to.

Naismith *et al.* (2004) states that m-learning can be used in
six basic ways:

- *As a quick feedback or reinforcement of a
  learning activity*
  One child-care tutor found that her group's attention was
  distracted during a session in which they were meant to be
  concentrating on a video. As an alternative, she placed a
  10-minute section of the video onto a set of PDAs. She
  then split the group into twos and asked them to review
  the video on the PDA and to comment on its content. As
  a result of the students being able to wind the video

backwards and forwards, she found that they could revisit aspects that they would have overlooked in a group situation and the level of learning was much deeper.

- *For investigations on the move or for games*
  A business tutor arranged for her students to visit a large nearby airport. The students had access to a PDA. They used the handwriting recognition facility on the PDA to write their notes as the airport manager gave a talk to them on the airport systems. The PDA automatically converted their written notes into typed text. Even though there were some mistakes in the translation, the students corrected these at a later stage. This saved them having to retype them later and the tutor found that in their written assignments the students had made much greater use of their notes than previously.

- *For use in the field or in a location such as within a museum*
  A land-based tutor was covering the subject of soil analysis in fields. He provided a PDA to groups of four students along with a handheld Global Positioning Systems (GPS) device. The students were then asked to provide a soil analysis report on a field and to use the PDA to record their results on a spreadsheet, along with the locations of their analysis sites, as determined using their GPS. They then had to plot this information onto a map and provide a soil analysis report on the field as a PowerPoint presentation. Using this technique, he then commented on the way they had produced the analysis and the validity of the sampling pattern.

- *To share information or to communicate in a collaborative learning activity*
  One group of students were split into groups of two and provided with a PDA. The PDA had a spreadsheet on it which they used to assess a workplace for hazards as defined by COSHH (Control of Substances Hazardous to Health) legislation. Although they each used the same spreadsheet, they were each asked to use a different worksheet and to record their results onto this worksheet. The results were then amalgamated in the next session and

a group assessment of the risks in the work environment was developed.

- *As a device the student carries with them for learning on the move*
  One tutor provided PDAs on short term-loan to his students in preparation for a plant identification assessment. The PDA had a set of information about various plants, including images of plants at various stages and their Latin names recorded as speech. The students could access this information whenever they had time to look at it, e.g. some reviewed this while they were coming into college on the bus.

- *As a support activity such as registers or for timetables*
  One college provided a set of PDAs to every tutor in a department. This was linked to the college's timetabling system and the latest register was automatically downloaded onto the PDA every evening. The staff simply took the PDAs off to the classroom and used them to register the students. Whenever the member of staff returned to their desk, they placed the PDA onto its docking station and the registers were uploaded onto the system. This saved the tutor having to do anything more than enter their registers once and ensured that the college had up-to-date registration information.

The above examples illustrate how tutors who have had access to a 'teaching set' of PDAs have introduced innovative ideas that promote learning in their subjects.

Mobile phones

Your students nearly all have mobile phones (and try to use them – even when you wish they wouldn't!), so can you use this technology to involve your students more? We should be seeing this as an opportunity to engage with our students, rather than as a problem. Texting (SMS) is an everyday thing to our students: we should be using this where we can. But how? I know texting isn't 'real English' but it allows us to meet some of our more problematic students on their own ground. Students see texting as a thing that tutors don't understand, let's prove them wrong!

For example, why not use text messages as part of a communications session to look at how the students might translate a phrase into texting to help convey the same message to a teenage audience. They could then look at some of their own text messages and rework them into standard English.

You can use a mobile phone to interact with your students – to provide extra hints for assignments that you have set, or to send out homework questions ready for their next sessions. If you are feeling really brave (and have the time), you could use them to set up question-and-answer sessions with your students. You don't have to be a texting wizard to do this: a number of sites allow you to harvest your students' messages and to send out your texts from the PC on your desk to all the students in a group at once.

Some colleges have set up systems which link their main server computer to a database of questions and other information and which then sends off a simple text-based quiz that the students can attempt, and get instant feedback from, via their mobiles.

Mobile-phone-based learning games are another possibility. Unfortunately, there are only a limited number of educational games available at the moment. Short multiple-choice quizzes can be very effective and, when presented along with good graphics to hold the student's interest, are very useful for repetitive practice activities. Sound-based quizzes also lend themselves effectively to use on mobile phones. The potential of this area of technology is rapidly developing as more and more students move from mobile phones onto smartphones.

Smartphones
These combine a full-featured mobile phone with the applications available on a PDA, and some even have a radio built in. Their main advantage is that they come already Internet-enabled. They use 3G mobile-phone technologies. The latest devices have the functionality of a PDA combined with the mobile and have an LCD TFT screen, a multi-megapixel camera, and offer integrated GPS. From a teaching perspective, this means they could have great potential, as they can deliver

video clips to your students' phones and allow both you and your students to send and receive video calls.

Smartphones and wireless handheld sales rose by 170 per cent year on year in the first part of 2005 in Europe and the Middle East whereas, by contrast, standard mobile phone shipments rose by only 11 per cent (Canalys 2005).

The relatively low cost of smartphones opens up the use of on-demand e-learning as a real possibility without vast amounts having to be spent on college infrastructures. E-learning devices such as these can also lead to off-site learning, with the student accessing both in-course and background information as a matter of course whenever and wherever they feel that they have time to devote to it.

MMS or picture messaging has a lot of potential, as it is now very easy to send images, audio clips and videos from one phone to another or to a website that will collect it. Imagine what could be done in terms of collaborative learning using this technology.

One example of the use of this is mediaBoard from CTAD. It allows you to set up a message board for a group of students. The students add comments not via their PCs but straight from their mobile phones using text messages (SMS) or via picture messages (MMS). The mediaBoard has a central image with zones on it. The zones can be locations on a map (showing people's faces, for example). Messages sent in to the mediaBoard are stored in the different sections. More information on this can be found at www.m-learning.org/mediaboard.shtml

The implications of using the technologies mentioned above for formal college structures is immense, as the student and their learning spaces become as mobile as the technology they have to hand.

A cautionary note

The holy grail is that learning becomes an integrated part of the students' everyday life, so thought needs to be given by departmental and senior management teams to facilitating these changes – a major challenge!

One tutor experimented with using a set of mobile devices to deliver 'anytime, anywhere' tuition to his students. He provided a blend of lectures reinforced with a series of tasks that the students could complete in their own time or during a nominally taught session at the college. The session was timetabled within the students' course, but the tutor did not provide a standard face-to-face classroom situation. He used the time to monitor, assess and provide feedback on the students' work and to be available to answer students' queries.

His biggest challenge was not getting the students to involve themselves in the system but to prevent his being timetabled to cover other sessions during this time, since he was viewed by his line manager as being sat at his computer and therefore not undertaking teaching. This is sometimes an aspect of e-learning which is forgotten by enthusiasts as they discover its huge potential. If you move down the e-learning route, you are still at the cutting edge of delivery and you must ensure that you have thought through the implications, not just for your students but for yourself. In many cases, your line managers will need persuading if you are taking a radical departure from the 'normal' delivery methods!

9 Guides for your journey

Sources of help

As you have seen, e-learning offers a wealth of options in terms of new kinds of teaching resources and new and exciting methods of delivery. With a little know how, you can very easily tailor and create your own unique e-learning experiences for your students. But what if you are absolutely new to using ILT or e-learning, where is the best place to start and where can you turn for advice and support? With so many things to consider, the idea of adopting any form of e-learning can seem very daunting, but it needn't be, because there is lots of support available.

 First of all, it is important to remember that you are not alone! Practitioners like yourself, right across the UK, are also trying new ways of incorporating e-learning into their learning delivery and there is a lot of help being made available to support this activity. So don't be deterred: your e-learning journey doesn't have to be a solo one – should you need help, you will surely find a number of guides to assist you along the way!

As a starting point, your own college is likely to have individual people or teams devoted to supporting its ILT and e-learning activity. What's more, you will find that there are also increasing numbers of external bodies that have been set up to support your adoption of e-learning at a practitioner level too.

Of course, you may not want to go outside of your college for help. You may feel most comfortable simply asking a colleague, but it is useful to know where you can turn to should you need to. What follows in this chapter are some useful details, Web addresses and starting points to help you get the support you need.

Help is close at hand

There are likely to be a number of internal sources of help within your college. Of course, the degree of available support will vary according to the size of the institution but a good starting place for e-learning advice might be your team of librarians or learning resource staff.

Learning resource staff

Earlier, we discussed the importance of using well-designed learning resources within your teaching, to help you to be able to get the most out of e-learning. Whether you decide to create your own materials or you want to know what other electronic learning resources exist, your college's librarians or learning resource staff should be able to help you. They will be aware of what resources exist within your college, what the institution is subscribed to and perhaps offer examples of ways in which these resources can be most effectively used by you in class. Depending on the size of your college's learning resource staff team, they may also be able to offer some support in terms of working with you to demonstrate how to use various resources with your students. For example, earlier in Chapter 5, we discussed using Infotrack with a group of media students. That is just one example of an activity that perhaps the learning resource staff would be happy to assist with.

IT support

Your college will inevitably have technical support staff whose focus will be on the setting up and maintenance of the IT systems used within the institution. They will provide front-line support and will be your first point of call for help with things such as software installations, hardware problems or malfunctions, network access and viruses. They should also be able to advise you on the compatibility of any assistive technology equipment that you might wish to use within your class. Your IT support team may provide other support services too; of course it will all depend on the size of the team and availability of resources within your institution.

ILT support

Unlike IT support whose role focuses on the installation and maintenance of IT systems, the ILT team will encourage the adoption and use of these systems and recommend ways that the available IT resources can be used more effectively. They can provide general help and advice on creating learning resources, designing for accessibility and offer guidance on the use of certain kinds of hardware and software. They will, therefore, be a good place to start if you are looking for help relating more specifically to IT-based resources that you might want to use within your class.

Help with content creation

Some colleges have dedicated teams who work within the area of ILT to remits more closely tied to content management and creation. They may be referred to as the content creation or materials development team.

It is becoming increasingly important for tutors to have their materials in Web-accessible formats for hosting on a VLE or an Intranet. (This was discussed more fully in Chapter 7.) To support this, some colleges will have small teams of people who, as well as creating resources themselves, will modify tutors' existing resources, repurposing them so that they are Web-enabled, reusable and more widely accessible. These teams can also advise on the use of a number of content creation tools that will help you to get started in creating your own e-learning resources from scratch.

These teams may offer several other kinds of support too. For example, if you have questions regarding copyright or need to know where you can source images and external resources for repurposing into your own class resources, this team may prove to be a good starting point.

External sources of help – e-learning support services

Outside of your college, there will also be a number of external agencies that are working together to support the national increase in the adoption of e-learning that is taking place within FE. Many of these bodies are public organizations funded by the government to ensure that the quality of e-learning provision in education is of a high standard. They are also keen to see a wider adoption of technology and strive to ensure that colleges share best practice and have national mechanisms in place for doing so.

JISC

The JISC is the main body for providing strategic guidance on the use of e-learning to the FE and HE sectors. It also provides a number of services that support the use of ILT and e-learning nationally. JISC has a very broad range of services that offer many different kinds of support in a number of key support areas. The complete list is extensive and new services are being added all the time as JISC's remit is extended. What follows are just some examples of the services currently available.

JISC network services
JISCMail is a national academic mailing list service that is available to support both the FE and HE community. To use the service, you can either find a list using JISCMail's search and browse facilities or be invited to join one by an existing member. Once you have been added to the list, you will automatically receive messages sent to the list by other members. New JISCMail lists are emerging all the time, a trend which reflects the increasing number of support groups that offer free and accessible peer support online. You can access the JISCmail services on the Web at www.jiscmail.ac.uk

JISC funds JANET (the Joint Academic Network), which connects all the UK's FE organizations, as well as HE and Research Councils. JANET is managed and operated by (UKERNA United Kingdom Education and Research Networking Association).

JISC development services
OSS Watch (Open Source Software Watch) provides advice concerning the adoption and use of free and open source

software (FOSS). It offers guidance on what kinds of open source software is available and how this might be used within FE. The OSS Watch website (and more recently its newly established Wiki) offers a wealth of materials to support the FE sector. It even has links which direct you to trusted sites where you download your own copies of open source software too. More information can be found on the OSS Watch website at

(a) www.osswatch.ac.uk

UKOLN (UK Office for Library Networking) is a centre of expertise in digital information management and is based at the University of Bath. It provides advice and services to the library, information, education and cultural heritage communities. You can learn more about its services on their website at

(a) www.ukoln.ac.uk

JISC expert services

Legality and copyright issues in the area of IT can be a complex area to say the least. So it is extremely helpful that JISC Legal Information Service provides guidance concerning legal compliance issues in ILT. Through workshops and its website, it offers information on how the law affects ICT users throughout the FE sector. You can learn more about the JISC legal services

(a) and access their website at www.jisclegal.ac.uk

Netskills

Based in the University of Newcastle, the Netskills team have been developing Internet training courses which have been successfully used by ACL and FE practitioners since 1995. They also run a regular series of face-to-face training workshops to support practitioners nationally. Details of their workshops and

(a) materials are available on their website at www.netskills.ac.uk

TASI

The Technical Advisory Service for Images provides support in the use and creation of digital images. Their three main areas of support include a website, an email helpdesk support service and a series of training programmes and workshops which they run across the UK. More information can be found on their

(a) website at www.tasi.ac.uk

JISC support services

The network of JISC Regional Support Centres (RSCs) support the implementation of the JISC strategy. They provide front-line support and work closely with practitioners in FE colleges to ensure they are fully aware of the full range of JISC services available to them. By working within the actual colleges, RSC teams are able to effectively identify ICT staff development needs and facilitate training that will support these needs. They also set up and maintain support networks amongst institutions both regionally and nationally, maximizing the benefits of having 13 RSCs across the UK. A full list of all the regional support centres with links to their websites can be accessed on the Web at www.jisc.ac.uk/index.cfm?name=rsc

JISC exemplars

In Chapter 5 we introduced the JISC Collections, resources that can be used to enrich education and research. But as a practitioner you may still want to know how you can use these resources and how they can be effectively mapped to your curriculum area. As a way of offering some guidance and inspiration, JISC has commissioned five exemplars which show examples of how several of these resources can be used by tutors to support their classroom activity. They also provide walk-throughs for a number of different scenarios relating to various qualifications.

These exemplars are available on the Web at http://restricted. jisc. ac.uk/exemplars_fe. There is restricted access and you must be working within an education institution to access these online. There are currently five exemplars covering the following subjects:

- History
- Leisure
- Hairdressing
- Business
- Skills for Life.

At the time of writing, JISC and the Department for Education and Skills (DfES) are compiling a series of case studies which show how practitioners have used the exemplars. They are also partnering in a study to evaluate the effectiveness of the exemplars, looking at how well they actually support the FE practitioner who wants ideas in how to implement e-learning in their teaching delivery.

JISC infoNet

JISC infoNet provides specialist information, communications and good practice support services to FE and HE, specifically as an advisory service for managers by promoting the effective strategic planning, implementation and management of ILT. More details are available on the Web at www.jiscinfonet. ac.uk

Ferl

Ferl was originally an acronym for Further Education Resources for Learning but its title is somewhat misleading, since it is now concerned with much more than just resources. Today Ferl is a source of advice and guidance for anyone involved in the use of ILT in the post-compulsory education sector. It is a Web-based service that is managed by British Educational Communications and Technology Agency (BECTA), the government's lead agency for ICT in education.

The Ferl website is structured around three main sections:

- policies and strategies
- teaching and learning
- technology for e-learning.

These contain a wealth of supporting materials for tutors, including key ILT documents and reports relevant to the Post-16 education sector. The site can also help you to decide which resources might be suitable to use as well as highlighting models of best practice for useful examples and ideas.

Below are examples of just some of the kind of things you are likely to find on Ferl:

- Reviews of websites and online resources. These are displayed in categories relating to individual subject areas making them easy to browse through for ideas.

- Case studies and lesson plans with materials that can be adapted for your own teaching.
- Articles that show you how to create your own resources for teaching and learning.
- Details of ILT-related events as well as ILT news stories from across the UK.

You can access the Ferl website at Ferl.becta.org.uk

NIACE

NIACE (National Institute of Adult Continuing Education) is a charity which aims to: 'support an increase in the total numbers of adults engaged in formal and informal learning in England and Wales. At the same time it takes positive action to improve opportunities and widen access to learning opportunities for those communities under-represented in current provision' (NIACE 2005).

It is the aim of NIACE to ensure that those who have benefitted least from education and training are given the best access to learning opportunities. The charity places particular emphasis on supporting those groups that are under-represented in education.

NIACE liaises with providers of Post–16 education and training as well as funding bodies and industry to ensure that all students' needs are represented across the sector. The charity also conducts research, and produces various publications – many of which are available on its website. NIACE arranges seminars, conferences and training events which support staff in Post-16 education and also encourage networking across the sector. It currently has offices based in Leicester (England) and Cardiff (Wales).

NIACE E-Guides

The E-Guides staff development programme was designed by NIACE to help ACL staff to develop the skills they needed to embed e-learning within their teaching. The programme also aims to support participants by showing them how to effectively cascade these new skills throughout their own organizations.

Based on the success of the initial phase of E-Guides training, the programme has now been extended to include library staff and there are also a number of e-guides based within colleges across the UK. Because the E-Guides programme was originally designed for the ACL sector, Aclearn, the part of BECTA that caters for ACL has materials to support E-Guides on its website. These include:

- An overview of the E-Guides programme, with details of how you can apply to become an E-Guide.
- Information on good practice in refining and developing e-learning skills.
- Useful resources to support E-Guides including several actively used message boards and lists of useful materials.

@ More details about NIACE are available on the Web at www.niace.org.uk and you can access the aclearn website at www.aclearn.net

LSN

The Learning and Skills Network (LSN) undertakes research training and consultancy to improve the quality of Post-16 education and training in the UK.

@ More details are available on the Web at www.lsn education.org.uk

ALT

ALT (Association for Learning Technology) seeks to bring together all those with an interest in the use of learning technology and has a membership of over 200 organizations and over 500 individuals. It has an FE as well as an HE focus. More

@ details are available on the Web at www.alt.ac.uk

Summary

As we have shown, there are lots of available sources of help, and lots of individuals willing to help to guide you in your e-learning journey. The Web itself has vast amounts of resources that are designed to support you, and show you how to implement e-learning in some of the most effective ways.

There are also many good mailing lists which, as well as keeping you up to date with developments in technology, also provide invaluable peer support. The old adage applies – two heads are better than one – and the success of so many discussion groups such as the JISC Curriculum Champions forum proves that this is the case!

As practitioners are encouraged to become more IT literate and innovative in their teaching methods and delivery, large sums of money are being invested in organizations that are willing to offer support in everything from content creation to the legalities of using ILT. As a result, if you need guidance, there is sure to be the help you need somewhere out there: the key lies in knowing the right place to look. Of course, every situation is unique, and so effective solutions will be individual ones, but here we have indicated a number of starting points.

So what's yet to come? In the next chapter we try a little crystal-ball gazing and take a short look at some possibilities for the near future.

10 What's on the horizon?

What's on its way

There is a steady blurring of the edges between what tutors are expecting to be able to do with desktop computers and laptops, and what they might be able to do in future with tablets, handhelds and even with mobile phones and MP3 players such as iPods. Students in their other guise as customers are demanding – and getting – devices and software which are increasingly focused on interoperability and compatibility. Mobile phones with not just inbuilt digital cameras but inbuilt MP3 players and even storage for their files on SD cards are now readily obtainable.

Access to the Internet is still steadily increasing and this has, in turn, led to a steady rise in the number of different devices that can link to the Web. As your students increasingly want to keep in touch both with their friends and relatives and with the information and services available via the Internet, the possibilities for different ways of communicating and for passing on and receiving information from them is growing enormously.

Many tutors in the not too distant past felt that the new technologies would lead to their students withdrawing into their own cyberspace and losing their motivation to interact with their fellow students. As the technology improves, however, it seems that the opposite is happening. Students are using the technology for increased informal communication and a lot of social interactivity is now happening through the technology itself. As tutors, we need to be aware of these developments and to have some idea of where they are likely to lead in the next few years. A survey in Finland showed that mobile TV is now watched for an average of 20 minutes each day on public transport. If you use public transport in the UK, you can't help but notice the increased number of people who have small DVD players which they use to while away their journey time, or who settle down to listen to their iPods for the journey.

Students are changing the way they view learning itself. They are no longer so willing to sit back and be lectured at by subject specialists who are the 'fountain of knowledge': they want to participate more in the development of their own knowledge. Fortunately, the bulk of what we, as tutors, do will still apply, but we need to use technology to enhance the ways in which we deliver teaching and learning. Tutors need a general awareness of what is available and an appreciation of how it can be adapted for delivery of learning.

Blended learning

Many colleges and training organizations will be increasingly using blended learning, which integrates traditional methods with e-learning techniques. The devices that students encounter out of the learning environment itself, such as mobile phone technologies, will be increasingly used as part of the learning process. As mobile phones become more like handheld computers, the possibilities for their use by tutors increases enormously.

The classroom changes from providing a point at which knowledge is delivered in a fairly rigid format to a home base for exploration, where the tutor integrates traditional work-based and classroom teaching with online communication, learning and instruction.

WiFi

In Chapter 4 we mentioned WiFi in the digital classroom and in Chapter 8 we discussed the use of WiFi as a driver of mobile 'anytime, anywhere' learning so where might it go next? As wireless technology continues to develop and transmission becomes more reliable and more widespread, devices that can connect to wireless networks will become the norm. This will become an essential part of both the student's and the tutor's toolkits. FE colleges and other organizations will increasingly make use of this facility to distribute small chunks of learning-on-demand to their students. But things might progress from there so that the student actively accumulates snippets of learning for his/her own use. As well as the traditional notes written onto notepads, it is possible already for students to record a lecture using their mobile phones and send it on to their friend who can't make it to the lecture. Or perhaps the institution records the lecture as a matter of course and uploads the recording onto a Web-blog so that the students can download it to view again at their leisure. This could also be linked into an online discussion on the subject matter.

Intelligent searching

As the Web continues to grow, so does the difficulty in finding the right things on it! Students and tutors increasingly need to be able to find relevant Web pages and to organize their lists of pages in such a way that they can easily retrieve the information again. Software applications for searching and finding the right sets of information are becoming available.

These range from desktop search 'bots' (automated pieces of software which roam the Net looking for information and which you can personalize to seek just your areas of interest), to cataloguing and search tools on college Intranets, to more specialized Web-search programs such as Google Scholar (http://scholar.google.com). Tutors will increasingly need to know how to use these facilities and how to integrate them into their teaching – how many of your students still go to the college library and look for information on the shelves in preference to searching for it on the Web? As tutors we are already finding the need to address the problems as well as the opportunities that the massive amounts of information available on the Web provide.

Games

Educational gaming is an expanding new area and can be used to great effect with students who are increasingly used to computer-based games. Even though they have always been used in education, games can now be used in differing ways by linking into the technology. Just as with more conventional games, learning technology-enhanced games need to be presented to the students in a structured way if they are to get maximum benefit from them.

Social networks and knowledge Webs

Tutors are discovering that social interactivity is just as possible over the Web as it is in face-to-face situations; even more so, in some cases, as tasks can be carried out asynchronously. The technology can be used to develop teamwork and enhance knowledge and understanding. Done correctly, the background context becomes irrelevant, as the task at hand takes over for the student and the message overtakes the medium. Wikis and blogs are becoming increasingly popular and can be used in a very constructive way to enhance learning. See http://wiki.org/wiki.cgi?What IsWiki and http://en.wikipedia.org/wiki/Blog, and www.sosig.ac.uk/socsciweek/blog

Electronic voting systems

These are being used within more and more institutions, as their price reduces and their versatility increases. These systems allow a class to vote on topics or a specific question and the results can be viewed on a screen. They are a good way of obtaining feedback and can be used to assess an individual's knowledge within a group situation since, provided you know who has a particular voting tablet then you can review their responses. But supposing you could link smartphones together as voting systems? The possibilities for this as a learning tool would be much greater. You could, for instance, produce a series of short videos or flash movies and allow the student to identify hazards in the workplace by selecting where they believe there is a hazard. The results could then be pooled and a group discussion could then follow on the various hazards identified and why they were perceived to be hazards.

WiMax and handhelds

Handheld computers/Smartphones (I have used a combined term deliberately as whatever appears over the next couple of years will be a mixture of both devices) are likely to come to the fore in a much greater way in the near future. The major problem of these losing their data as batteries go flat will be overcome by the use of hard drives such as those used in MP3 players. As WiFi hotspots increase around the country, there will be much more opportunity to integrate them into a learning experience out of the institution. Suppose, for instance, a group of students visit an art gallery and point their handhelds at a painting which then supplies them with information about the artist that is also relevant to their current course? The handheld computer could use the screen to highlight various areas of importance in the painting and, as well as providing an audio explanation, also download a text version that the student can access later for use as background for an assignment.

New WiMax technology could provide direct-to-Internet connections from the handhelds as it has a very fast download rate and a range of several kilometres. Wireless roaming of cities, a technique that is already being used in the tourist industry in some countries, would then be possible for student groups. The tutor could provide access to a whole range of text, images, videos and sounds that could enhance learning and add interest to their courses. If this sounds far-fetched, I was at a conference two years ago at which we were listening to the opening speaker talk about Vannevar Bush, who is credited with coming up with many of the outline ideas for the Worldwide Web. My colleague became intrigued with this so he linked his handheld PC to his mobile phone, downloaded the article that Bush wrote, and had it available to view within a couple of minutes!

So have a go!

Whatever new device comes along, you can be sure that a large percentage of your students will probably have had a good look at it before you, as a tutor, get around to adapting it for educational purposes. However, I don't see a problem with this, as there will always be some staff who will experiment with the latest devices and some devices which simply will not take off in the way that they were expected to. Students will not be looking at the devices in the way that you will be looking at them, but will appreciate your attempts to use them as part of their learning experience.

We have not covered all aspects of e-learning in this book and there will inevitably be some aspects that certain staff hold dear to their hearts which we have missed altogether. However, we hope that you have found this overview useful and that it has opened your eyes to the vast range of learning opportunities that can be made available by embracing e-learning within your teaching delivery. The future is hard to predict and it may be that the areas we have concentrated on are not as promising as they currently seem to be. In ten years time someone may look back at sections of this book and think 'Wow, they were certainly going up a dead-end there!' This is a risk we have to take, since, as with buying a computer, if you wait until you can afford the latest model, you will never get around to buying one! If you wait until everyone else is using e-learning as part of their delivery, you will never get started. The time to have a go is now – I can remember a staff member who said that whiteboards and coloured pens would never take over from chalk!

Further resources

References

Canalys.com, 2005, 'Mobile Device Trends 2005', www.canalys.com/reports/index.htm

Ferl, 2003, 'Learning objects under the spotlight', Bob Powell, Technology for E-Learning > Learning Objects, accessed 30 May 2006, ferl.becta.org.uk/display.cfm?resID=5283

Ferl, 2005, Technology for E-Learning > Advice > Content Tools, accessed 18 April 2006, ferl.becta.org.uk/display.cfm?page=869 &variation=101

Fischer Family Trust, 2005, 'Impact of e-learning on GCSE results of 105,617 students, 2004', SAM Learning, accessed 18 April 2006, www.samlearning.com/docs/measureable_improvement/2005–02% 20Impact%20Report%20Update.html

Kukulska-Hulme, Agnes, 2005, 'Current Uses of Wireless and Mobile Learning', Open University, accessed 18 April 2006, www.jisc.ac.uk/uploaded_documents/Current%20Uses%20FINAL %202005.doc

Naismith, L., Lonsdale, P., Vavoula, G., Sharples, M., 2004, 'Mobile Technologies and Learning', nestafuturelab.org.uk, accessed 18 April 2006, www.nestafuturelab.org/research/lit_reviews.htm # lr11

Naughton, John, 1999, *A Brief History of the Future: The Origins of the Internet*, Weidenfeld & Nicolson, London

NMC: The New Media Consortium, 2005, 'Horizon Report 2005', accessed 18 April 2006, www.nmc.org/horizon

NIACE, 2005, accessed 30 May 2006, www.niace.org.uk/organisation

Office of National Statistics, 2002, 'Activities Undertaken on the Computer at Home by 11–18 year-olds, Autumn 2002: Social Trends 34', accessed 18 April 2006, www.statistics.gov.uk/StatBase/ssdataset.asp?vlnk=7206

Office of National Statistics, 2005, 'Internet Connectivity', accessed 18 April 2006, www.statistics.gov.uk/pdfdir/intc0805.pdf

Stead, G., Sharpe, B, Anderson, P., Cyche, L., Philpott, M., 2006,

'Emerging Technologies for Learning, BECTA', accessed 18 April 2006, www.becta.org.uk/corporate/publications/publications_detail. cfm?show=latest&orderby=title_asc&letter=ALL&pubid=321

Websites mentioned in the text

http://corporate.digitalbrain.com/index.php
http://edina.ac.uk/digimap
http://edina.ac.uk/eig/index.shtml
http://eebo.chadwyck.com/home
http://ferl.becta.org.uk
http://ferl.becta.org.uk/display.cfm?catID=1
http://http://ferl.becta.org.uk/display.cfm?page=869&variation=101
http://fronter.co.uk/uk
http://moodle.org
http://reports.mintel.com
http://restricted.jisc.ac.uk/exemplars_fe
http://webxact.watchfire.com
http://www.abilitynet.org.uk/content/home.htm
http://www.abilitynet.org.uk/myway
http://www.acce-lerator.net
http://www.acleam.net
http://www.alt.ac.uk
http://www.angellearning.com
http://www.bbc.co.uk/learning
http://www.becta.org.uk/corporate/publications/publications_detail.cfm?
    show=latest&orderby=title_asc&letter=ALL&pubid=321
http://www.blackboard.com/uki
http://www.britannica.co.uk
http://www.channel4.com/learning
http://www.cmeducation.co.uk/HTML/index.htm
http://www.coursemanager.com
http://www.creativeclub.co.uk
http://www.desire2learn.com
http://www.ecollege.com
http://www.eduserv.org.uk/chest
http://www.galeuk.com/jisc/index.htm
http://www.geoprojects.co.uk
http://www.helpisathand.gov.uk/resources/teaching-learning/groups/
    disabilities/tips
http://www.horizonwimba.com
http://www.jenzabar.com

http://www.jisc.ac.uk/index.cfm?name=rsc
http://www.jisc.ac.uk/uploaded_documents/Current%20Uses%20
    FINAL %202005.doc
http://www.jiscinfonet.ac.uk
http://www.jisclegal.ac.uk
http://www.jiscmail.ac.uk
http://www.knowuk.co.uk
http://www.learnwise.com
http://www.LSNeducation.org.uk
http://www.m-learning.org/mediaboard.shtml
http://www.nestafuturelab.org/research/lit_reviews.htm #lr11
http://www.netskills.ac.uk
http://www.newsbank.com/UK/nbnp_uk.html
http://www.niace.org.uk
http://www.nln.ac.uk/Materials
http://www.nmc.org/horizon
http://www.oss-watch.ac.uk
http://www.plateau.com
http://www.rdn.ac.uk
http://www.reload.ac.uk
http://www.samlearning.com/docs/measurable_improvement/
    2005–02%20 impact%20Report%20Update.html
http://www.statistics.gov.uk/pdfdir/intc0805.pdf
http://www.statistics.gov.uk/StatBase/ssdataset.asp?vink=7206
http://www.tasi.ac.uk
http://www.techdis.ac.uk
http://www.techdis.ac.uk/index.php?p=1_20051905100544
http://www.techdis.ac.uk/resources/sites/staffpacks/index.xml
http://www.teknical.com/products/virtual_campus_v5.htm
http://www.theacademiclibrary.com
http://www.ukoln.ac.uk
http://www.vts.rdn.ac.uk
http://www.webct.com/entrypage

Index